Editor
Emily R. Smith, M.A. Ed.

Editorial Project Manager
Elizabeth Morrris, Ph. D.

Editor-in-Chief
Sharon Coan, M.S. Ed.

Cover Artist
Lesley Palmer

Art Coordinator
Denice Adorno

Imaging
James Edward Grace
Alfred Lau

Production Manager
Phil Garcia

Acknowledgements
Microsoft® Word™ is a registered
trademark of Microsoft
Corporation.

Publisher
Mary D. Smith, M.S. Ed.

Microsoft® Word™
Simple Projects

Challenging

Author

Jan Ray, Ed. D.

Teacher Created Resources, Inc.
6421 Industry Way
Westminster, CA 92683
www.teachercreated.com
ISBN-1-57690-730-9

©*2001 Teacher Created Resources, Inc.*
Reprinted, 2005
Made in U.S.A.

Table of Contents

Introduction

Welcome to *Microsoft Word*: **Simple Projects—Challenging**. You hold in your hands a book that is designed to help you use *Microsoft Word* in the classroom with your students. It contains language arts, mathematics, social studies, and science projects that incorporate the use of *Microsoft Word*. The projects were developed for fifth- through eighth-grade teachers and their students.

Microsoft Word is a word processing software application designed to help you produce letters, memos, reports, newsletters, brochures, and many other documents. Although *Microsoft Word* was originally designed for use in the business world, you will soon discover how nicely it can be applied to the field of education. If you are not familiar with the basics of using *Microsoft Word*, I recommend that you purchase and work through the lessons in ***Microsoft Word* for Terrified Teachers** first (also published by Teacher Created Resources). ***Microsoft Word* for Terrified Teachers** provides you with step-by-step instructions for learning *Microsoft Word*. It also includes some great project ideas.

Software Used for This Book

All the *Microsoft Word* files and templates in this book were created using *Microsoft Word 2000* for Windows. So, the screen shots, menus, etc. might look a little different if you are using a different version or platform. However, you should have no difficulty if you are using a Macintosh computer or a different version of *Word*. The files and templates can be used in *Microsoft Word 95*, *Microsoft Word 97-98*, or *Microsoft Word 2000*.

About the Projects

In this book you will find 19 projects that you can complete with your students. Each project is presented as follows:

Project Description

In this section you are provided with a brief description of the project, allowing you a quick overview of the process and culminating product.

Hardware and Software Needed

In this section you are provided information about the hardware and software you will need to complete the project. Sometimes optional hardware and software are also listed, allowing you to choose the method you prefer for working through the project with your students.

Materials Needed

In this section all the materials and supplies you need to complete the project are listed, including those that apply to alternate methods.

CD-ROM Files

In this section you are provided with a list of the teacher resource files, student activity sheets, template files, presentation files, and more that are associated with the projects. The list includes the filename of each piece, so you can readily retrieve it from the CD-ROM.

Introducing the Project

In this section you are provided with ideas for preparing your students for the project.

Introduction

About the Projects *(cont.)*

Producing the Project

In this section you are provided with instructions for producing the project with your students.

Presenting the Project

In this section you are provided with ideas for publishing the project.

Additional Project Ideas

In this section ideas for extending the project are listed. Many times, ideas for parallel, supplementary, or alternative projects are also provided.

Additional Resources

In this section you are provided with several resources that will support, supplement, or expand your project. Many of the resources are found on the Internet. In order to avoid typing in the lengthy address of each Internet site, an *Additional Resources* file is provided on the CD-ROM [filename: addrsorc.doc]. The file lists all the resources from every project in this book. Resources that are Internet sites can be easily identified on the CD-ROM because they are in bright blue text and underlined. (After they are launched, the text turns bright purple.) They have been saved as hyperlinks so you can simply click on any Internet address and you will automatically go there. (Be sure to have your Web browser open and running in the background before you click.)

About the CD-ROM

Turn to the back of this book and you will find a CD-ROM. Please note that the CD-ROM does not contain *Microsoft Word*. You must have *Microsoft Word* already loaded onto your computer system prior to starting the projects in this book.

This CD-ROM does contain 91 project-related files. An index of the CD-ROM files can be found starting on page 93. You will find teacher resource files, student activity sheets, template files, presentation files, and more on the CD-ROM.

You can access a file on the CD-ROM by placing the CD in the CD-ROM drive of your computer system. Since accessing the CD is just a little bit different within *Microsoft Windows* than it is on the Macintosh, you will find separate directions for each below.

If you are using **Windows**, double-click on the **My Computer** icon on your desktop. At the **My Computer** window, double-click on the icon representing the CD-ROM drive, such as **D:** or **E:**. (You may also see the name of the CD [tcm_2730] right next to the CD drive label. That's helpful!) At the **tcm_2730** window, you will see a list of all the files on the CD-ROM. Just scroll down until you find the file you want and double-click on the file to open it. Windows will automatically launch the software application that is associated with the file.

Introduction

If you are using a **Macintosh** system, double-click on the CD icon that is on your desktop. Just scroll down until you find the file you want and double-click on the file to open it. The system will automatically launch the application that is associated with the file.

About File Management

Managing all the files that you create and use on the computer system can become overwhelming—even frustrating. So, I thought you might want a little help with this very important aspect of using the computer.

Before beginning to use this book, create a folder on your desktop for all the files. Since creating a folder is just a little bit different within Windows than it is on the Macintosh, you will find separate directions for each below.

If you are using **Windows**—click your right mouse button in any blank area on the Windows desktop. A pop-up menu will appear. Select **New**. Another pop-up menu will appear. Select **Folder**.

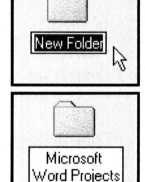

A new folder will appear on your desktop with a folder label below it. The folder label reads *New Folder*, but it is highlighted, awaiting your changes. Simply begin typing a new label or name for this folder, such as *Microsoft Word Projects*. Then double-click on any blank area of the Windows desktop to complete the process.

If you are using a **Macintosh** computer—at the desktop, click on the **FILE** menu and pull down to *New Folder*. When the new folder appears on the desktop, simply change the name from *untitled folder* to *Microsoft Word Projects*.

Now, whenever you access a file from the CD-ROM or create a new file on your own, you can save it in the *Microsoft Word Projects* folder on your desktop. You may want to make similar folders on all the computers in your classroom, so that as students create files for the projects, they know where to save their work as well.

Special Note: All the files from the CD-ROM are read only. (That's why it is called a CD-ROM—ROM means read-only memory.) You cannot take a file from the CD-ROM, change it, and save it back to the CD-ROM. (Well, you can, but you will lose any changes you have made.) So, as you retrieve a file from the CD-ROM, use the *Save As* command under the **FILE** menu of whatever software application you are using to save the file to a new location, such as your newly created *Microsoft Word Projects* folder on the desktop.

Introduction

About File Management *(cont.)*

Here's a little bit more of an explanation. When you have a CD-ROM file open, click on the **FILE** menu and pull down to *Save As*. For **Windows**, in the *Save As* window, at the **Save in:** command line, click on the drop-down menu button. The drop-down menu displays a list of all the places where you can navigate to save your file.

Select **Desktop**. (If you don't see **Desktop** on the drop-down menu, you may have to scroll up. **Desktop** is always at the top of the list.) Once you have **Desktop** selected, you should see your *Microsoft Word Projects* folder. Double-click on the folder to open it.

Save As

Save in: Desktop

Microsoft Word Projects should now appear in the **Save in:** command line. And that's where you want your file to go! Name or rename the file, if necessary. Then, click on the **Save** button, and you're done.

For the **Macintosh**, after you click on the **FILE** menu and pull down to *Save As,* navigate to the **Desktop**, and open your *Microsoft Word Projects* folder. Name or rename the file, if necessary. Then click **Save**.

Save As

Save in: Microsoft Word Projects

Now you know where your file will be the next time you want to use it. Plus, you can create folders within this folder (maybe one for each project) to help you stay even more organized as you work through project after project.

Adapting Projects to Meet Your Needs

As a teacher, I know you are a master at adapting lessons to meet the needs of your students. Well, feel free to do the same with the projects that follow. For example, in the Creating Fraction Games activity, you may be more concerned about your students who still don't know their multiplication facts and decide to adapt the activity by having your students create multiplication fact family games instead. So go ahead, open the *Microsoft Word* files and change the projects to meet your students' needs.

When you use the *Microsoft Word* template files from the CD-ROM, feel free to change the document formatting to what you like best. Adapt the breadth and depth of the projects and their documents to match the ability levels of your students.

In Conclusion

Well, that's it for your quick introduction to *Microsoft Word*: **Simple Projects—Challenging**. I hope you enjoy using the *Microsoft Word* projects with your students as much as I have enjoyed developing them for you.

Your feedback on this book is always welcome. You can contact the publisher or me with your comments, suggestions, and more through the *Teacher Created Resources* Web site at **http://www.teachercreated.com** or **drjanray@hotmail.com**. Plus, I would love to see some of your finished *Microsoft Word* projects!

Iconic Story Writing

Project Description

In this activity, students select graphics from the *Microsoft Clip Gallery*. Students

 their short stories, making sure they incorporate the selected graphics. Students

 their stories to share with others.

Hardware and Software Needed

For this activity, you will need your computer system and *Microsoft Word*.

Materials You Will Need

Although students will be using the *Microsoft Clip Gallery*, you may want to gather other clip art CD-ROMs for them to use as an alternative.

CD-ROM Files

Name	Description	Filename
The Little Lost Kitten	Iconic story sample	lostkitn.doc
Iconic Story Template	Iconic story template	icontemp.doc

Introducing the Project

Explain to students that an icon is a picture or image that represents something. For example, the wastebasket on the computer screen represents the Recycle Bin. Discuss other icons that the students see in the classroom or in their everyday lives and what the icons represent.

If you choose, show students the iconic story *The Lost Little Kitten* that is shown on the following page. *The Lost Little Kitten* is also available on the CD-ROM [filename: lostkitn.doc].

Iconic Story Writing *(cont.)*

The wise old [owl] said, "Follow your [heart] [kitten]. It will lead you home to your [kitten]." "I will follow my [heart]." "I will try my best," said the little [kitten]. Little [kitten] closed his eyes and thought about his [heart]. He could feel so much love for her in his [heart] that he almost started crying again. "No more tears," the little [kitten] said to himself. "I must be brave!" Then little [kitten] scampered in the direction his [heart] told him to go. Soon he saw his [cat]. That [heart] made little [kitten] very, very happy!

The Little Lost Kitten

By
Sarah Jean

Once upon a time there was a little [kitten]. The little [kitten] loved to play in the [flower] and sleep in the warm [sun]. One day the little [kitten] got lost. He cried and cried. "Meow! Meow! Meow! Where is my [cat]?" He cried and cried. A wise old [owl] heard him crying. The wise old [owl] asked, "What is wrong, little [kitten]? Are you okay?" "No!" the little [kitten] answered sadly. "I am lost!"

Iconic Story Writing *(cont.)*

Producing the Project

Have students launch *Microsoft Word* and insert five graphics across the tops of their pages.

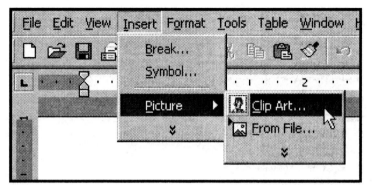

Here's How:

- Click on the **INSERT** menu, pull down to *Picture*, and select **Clip Art**.

- At the **Insert Clip Art** window, navigate through the categories until you find an image you like.

- Click on the image and then the **Insert** button.

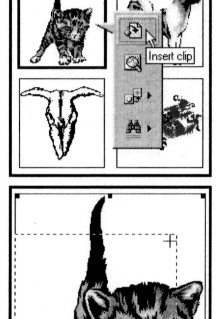

- Close or minimize the **Insert Clip Art** window to return to your *Microsoft Word* document.

- Click on the graphic to select it. A frame and resize buttons should appear around the graphic.

- Move your cursor over one of the resize buttons. When you do, your cursor will change from an insertion line to a two-headed resize arrow.

- Click, hold, and drag the resize arrow (which actually turns into a crosshair) to make the image smaller.

- Release when the image is approximately one inch wide. (Remember, you have to get five images across the top of the page!)

- Click to the right of the image to deselect it.

- Press the spacebar on your keyboard one or two times to allow just a bit of space before entering the next image.

- Repeat this process, inserting four more images. You may need to resize the images several times to fit all five across the top of the page. It's good practice! You may also want to adjust the spacing between the images so that they look as equidistant as possible.

Once the images are in place, have students press **<Enter>** or **<Return>** a few times on their keyboards and begin writing the short stories using the selected graphics. Allow students to include other graphic images whenever possible.

Special Note: Students can copy and paste the in-text images from those at the top rather than returning to the *Microsoft Clip Gallery*; however, the in-text images will have to be made smaller. If the same images are used again, have the students copy and paste from already existing in-text images, so they will not have to resize every time.

Iconic Story Writing *(cont.)*

Producing the Project *(cont.)*

When students are done writing, have them return to the tops of their pages and insert appropriate titles and bylines. Students should center their titles and byline text. They can make the title text and byline text bold. Students may also change the font for their titles to a larger size (such as 16 point) and the font for their bylines to a medium size (such as 14 point).

Guide students as to how and where you would like them to save their iconic stories. Allow students to print their iconic stories and revise them as necessary.

Special Note: To eliminate the need for formatting, there is an *Iconic Story Template* available on the CD-ROM for you to use with your students [filename: icontemp.doc]. It has spaces marked for students to insert their graphics, titles, bylines, and beginning text.

Presenting the Project

- Have students share their iconic stories with each other or with another class. The stories can be read aloud by their authors or by peers.

- Post the iconic stories to your classroom Web page.

- Let students e-mail their iconic stories to family members and friends.

- Hang the iconic stories on a bulletin board or wall space in your classroom.

- Display the iconic stories in the hallway outside of your classroom for others to read and enjoy.

Additional Project Ideas

- Make holiday cards with iconic greetings, poems, and messages.

- For a change of pace, have students write their weekly spelling sentences using graphic images.

Additional Resources

- If your students are having difficulty finding just the right images in the *Microsoft Clip Gallery* on your computer system, open your Web browser and have them click on **Clips Online** within the **Insert Clip Art** window. They will automatically be taken to the *Microsoft Design Gallery* Web site. This site has over 120,000 graphic images and sounds from which they can choose. Students simply type in a search word, such as *cats*, and click on the **Go** button. Associated images will appear. Students can scroll through the images and select some for downloading. When downloaded, the images will automatically be placed in your computer system's *Microsoft Clip Gallery*. For direct access, the site address is:

  http://office.microsoft.com/clipart/

Open House Announcement

Project Description

In this activity, students create their own Open House announcement, informing family and friends of the "who, what, when, where, how, and why" associated with this event. Students desktop publish their announcements in *Microsoft Word*.

Hardware and Software Needed

For this activity, you will need your computer system and *Microsoft Word*.

Materials You Will Need

You will need the information about an upcoming school event, such as the Open House, to share with your students.

CD-ROM Files

Name	Description	Filename
Twin Peaks School Open House Announcement	Open House Announcement Sample	openhous.doc
Planning Our Open House Announcement	Student activity sheets	planopen.doc
Writing Process Tracking Sheet for the Open House Announcement	Student activity sheet	writproc.doc

Introducing the Project

Tell students that they will be the authors of this year's Open House announcements. If you choose, share with students the sample announcement—*Twin Peaks School Open House Announcement*—that is shown on the following page and is also available on the CD-ROM [filename: openhous.doc].

Review with students an author's purpose for writing, such as to entertain, to persuade, to describe, or to inform. Explain to the students how announcements, such as their Open House announcements, can be a form of writing that addresses all of these purposes. Their Open House announcements can **entertain** if they catch a person's eye, encouraging him or her to read on. Their Open House announcements can **persuade** someone to attend because of the interesting or exciting events listed. Their Open House announcements can **describe** the "who, what, when, where, how, and why" of the occasion. Their Open House announcements can **inform** readers of special events, telephone numbers, and instructions.

Open House Announcement *(cont.)*

Everyone is welcome at the Twin Peaks School!

OPEN HOUSE

Monday, September 14

6:30–8:30 P.M.

- Meet the teachers, students, other parents, and new friends
- Visit the expanded library
- See our new computer labs
- Snack on free desserts and drinks in the lunchroom
- Sign up to win one of ten door prizes in the principal's office
- Follow the maps to your child's room to view student projects and the curriculum
- Take your "little ones" to the gym for free childcare while you visit

Need more information?

Call 888-888-8888

This event is sponsored by the Twin Peaks PTSA

Open House Announcement *(cont.)*

Planning Our Open House Announcement

The "Who, What, When, Where, How, and Why" of Our Open House

The Five Ws and One H	Questions Related to the Five Ws and One H	Answers to the Questions	Are the Answers Reflected in Your Open House Announcement?
Who?	1. Who is conducting the Open House? 2. Who is attending the Open House?		
What?	1. What will visitors do at the Open House? 2. What will visitors learn at the Open House? 3. What are the "special events" at the Open House?		
When?	1. What date is the Open House? 2. What night is the Open House? 3. What time is the Open House?		
Where?	1. Where is the Open House? 2. Where should visitors go when they arrive at the Open House?		
How?	1. How will visitors benefit from attending the Open House? 2. How will visitors know where to go when they arrive at school? 3. How much does the Open House cost?		
Why?	1. Why is your school conducting an Open House? 2. Why should visitors come to the Open House?		

Open House Announcement *(cont.)*

Introducing the Project *(cont.)*

Help students determine who the readers of the Open House announcements might be, including fellow students, teachers, administrators, parents, grandparents, other family members, neighbors, friends, and more. Keeping this in mind, ask students what information the readers might need to help them decide whether or not to attend the Open House. Point out to students that one way to make sure the readers have all of the information they need is to use the traditional Five Ws and One H—"who, what, when, where, how, and why"—method.

Provide students with the *Planning Our Open House Announcement* activity sheet that is shown on the previous page to help them gather and formulate all the "who, what, when, where, how, and why" information they will need to complete the Open House announcements. The *Planning Our Open House Announcement* activity sheet file is also available on the CD-ROM [filename: planopen.doc].

Producing the Project

Once the *Planning Our Open House Announcement* activity sheet is complete, have students:

- Open *Microsoft Word*.

- Change the margins for the document to .75 inches on the top, bottom, left, and right, so that there is more workspace.

- **Here's How:**

  - On Windows machines, click on **FILE** and pull down to *Page Setup*. On a Macintosh, it's under **FORMAT—*Document***

  - At the **Page Setup** window, click on the **Margins** tab, bringing it to the forefront if it is not already there.

  - Change the **Top, Bottom, Left,** and **Right** margins to .75 inches, and click **OK**.

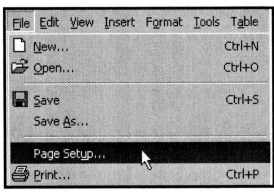 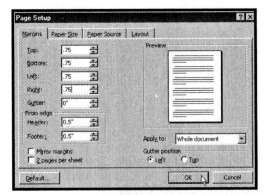

- Insert graphics that represent the Open House events.

- **Here's How:**

  - At the **Insert Clip Art** window, navigate through the categories until you find an image you like.

  - Click on the image and then the **Insert** button.

  - Close or minimize the **Insert Clip Art** window to return to your *Microsoft Word* document.

Open House Announcement *(cont.)*

- Resize the graphics so they look visually pleasing on the Open House announcements.
- **Here's How:**
  - Click on the graphic to select it. A frame and resize buttons should appear around the graphic.
  - Move your cursor over one of the resize buttons. When you do, your cursor will change from an insertion line to a two-headed resize arrow.

  - Click, hold, and drag the resize arrow (which actually turns into a crosshair) to make the image smaller.
  - Release when the image is the size you wish.
  - Click off the image to deselect it.
- Change the wrapping style of the graphics so that they can be placed on a page independent of the text. (The default setting puts graphics in line with text.)
- **Here's How:**
  - Click on the graphic to select it.
  - On Windows machines, right-click your mouse to get a pop-up menu and select **Format Picture**.
  - On Macintosh machines, click on the **FORMAT** menu and pull down to *Picture*.
  - At the **Format Picture** window, click on the **Layout** (or **Wrapping**) tab to bring it to the forefront if it is not already there.
  - Under **Wrapping style**, click on **Square**. Then click **OK** to return to your picture.

- Type in normal text as you wish, changing the text alignment and font face, font size, and font attributes to your liking.

Open House Announcement *(cont.)*

Producing the Project *(cont.)*

- Insert text boxes as you wish.

- **Here's How:**

  - Display the **Drawing Toolbar** if it is not already showing. (To display the **Drawing Toolbar**, click on the **VIEW** menu, pull down to *Toolbars*, and then select **Drawing**. The **Drawing Toolbar** will appear at the bottom of your document window.)

  - Click on the **Text Box** button on the **Drawing Toolbar**.

  - Click and drag the text box to the size you wish.

  - Click inside the text box and enter the text you desire.

  - Then click outside the text box to deselect it.

  - You can always click on the text box again and move it to a new location.

- Insert WordArt as you wish.

- **Here's How:**

  - Click on the **WordArt** button on the **Drawing Toolbar**.

  - At the **WordArt Gallery** window, select a **WordArt style** and click **OK**.

  - At the **WordArt Text** window, begin typing the text you want displayed.

  - Modify the font type, size, and attributes of the text you typed, if you desire.

  - Click **OK** when you are finished.

  - Once the WordArt appears on your Open House announcement, resize and move the WordArt just as you would a graphic.

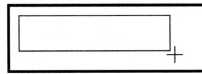

Open House Announcement *(cont.)*

- You may also want to include bulleted lists of items as you see on the sample *Twin Peaks School Open House Announcement.* Position your cursor on the line where you would like your text to appear and click on the **Bullets** button on the **Formatting Toolbar.** When you are done entering bulleted items on your Open House announcement, simply click on the **Bullets** button again to stop the bullets.

Since the Open House announcements will be published outside of your classroom, consider having students edit and revise their work until their Open House announcements are "picture perfect."

Presenting the Project

You should have a nice variety of Open House announcements to share with the world. Here are some ideas for distribution:

- Post them throughout the school.

- Send them home with students.

- Post them to your classroom or school Web page.

Additional Project Ideas

- Have students make the next announcements for your school book fair, science fair, carnival, play, or music festival.

Additional Resources

- If you choose to use the writing process with this project there is a *Writing Process Tracking Sheet* available for you and your students. It is shown on the following page and is also available on the CD-ROM [filename: writproc.doc]. This *Writing Process Tracking Sheet* is designed for peer review at the editing and proofreading stages. There is an author sign-off for prewriting, two peer editing passes with author revisions, one peer proofreading pass with an author revision, a teacher check with author last-minute fixes, and, of course, final publication. If you decide to use this *Writing Process Tracking Sheet,* feel free to modify it to align to the writing process you normally use in your classroom.

Open House Announcement *(cont.)*

Writing Process Tracking Sheet
for the
Open House Announcement

Name of Author: _____

Date	Stage	Author Sign-off	Reviewer Sign-off	Comments
	Prewriting			Finished the *Planning Our Open House Announcement* activity sheets.
	Drafting			
	First Editing Pass			
	First Revision			
	Second Editing Pass			
	Second Revision			
	Proofreading Pass			
	Final Revision			
	Teacher Check			
	Last-Minute Fixes			Yeah!
	Final Printing for Publication			

Super Spelling Triangles

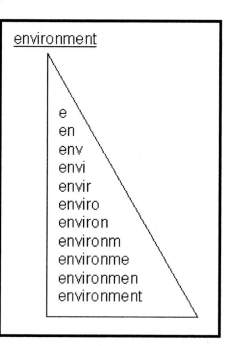

Project Description

In this activity, students practice keyboarding their spelling words as triangles. First, students type one spelling word as a reference. Next, students begin shaping the spelling word into a triangle by typing one letter, going to the next line and typing two letters, going to the next line and typing three letters, and so on. When the spelling word is completely typed, students have a spelling triangle! Then, using the *Microsoft Word* AutoShapes feature, students outline their work, displaying the right triangle they have shaped with the progressive typing of the spelling word.

Hardware and Software Needed

For this activity, you will need your computer system and *Microsoft Word*.

Materials You Will Need

For this activity, your students will need a list of spelling words for making their spelling triangles.

CD-ROM Files

Name	Description	Filename
My Spelling Triangles Sample	Sample student file	spellsam.doc
My Spelling Triangles Template	Student file template	spelltem.doc

Introducing the Project

Explain to students that they will be creating spelling triangles. If you choose, show students the *My Spelling Triangles Sample* that is shown on the following page. The *My Spelling Triangles Sample* file is also available on the CD-ROM [filename: spellsam.doc].

Provide students with their spelling lists and demonstrate how to create spelling triangles.

Here's How:

1. Open a new *Microsoft Word* document.

2. Enter the title of the document, such as *My Spelling Triangles*.

3. Center the title by selecting (highlighting) it, and clicking on the **Align Center** button on the **Formatting Toolbar**.

4. While the title is still selected, make it bold by clicking on the **Bold** button on the **Formatting Toolbar**.

Super Spelling Triangles *(cont.)*

Introducing the Project *(cont.)*

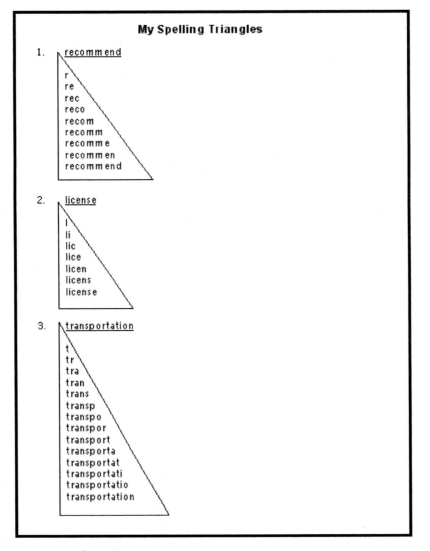

5. While the title is still selected, make the font a size or two larger (such as 14 point or 16 point) than the normal text (usually 12 point) by clicking the **Font Size** drop-down menu and selecting a larger font face size.

6. When you are done formatting the title, click to the right of it to deselect it.

7. Press **<Enter>** or **<Return>** a few times on your keyboard to provide some space between the title and the spelling words and triangles.

8. Before typing, check the text alignment, making sure your cursor is flush left rather than centered on the page. If it is still centered, change it now by clicking the **Align Left** button on the **Formatting Toolbar**.

9. Before typing, check the font size, making sure it is 12 point. If it is still 14 point or 16 point, change it now by clicking on the **Font Size** drop down menu on the **Formatting Toolbar** and selecting 12.

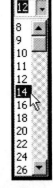

Super Spelling Triangles *(cont.)*

10. Before typing, check the font attribute, making sure that **Bold** is turned off. If it is still turned on, click the **Bold** button on the **Formatting Toolbar** to deselect this font attribute.

11. If you choose to number your spelling words, type the number 1, type a period (.), and then press the **<Tab>** key.

12. Type the first spelling word, such as *environment*. **Bold** or underline the spelling word so that it stands out.

13. Press **<Enter>** or **<Return>** once to start a new line.

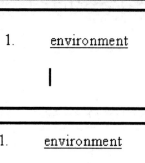

14. If the *Microsoft Word* **AutoFormat** feature indents the number 1 and inserts a number 2, don't panic. Simply click on the **EDIT** menu and pull down to ***Undo AutoFormat***. Your number 1 should return to its flush left position and the number 2 should disappear.

15. Press **<Enter>** or **<Return>** again to provide some additional space.

16. Press **<Tab>** to indent your cursor, aligning it with the first letter of the spelling word.

17. Type the first letter of the spelling word, such as *e*, and press **<Enter>** or **<Return>** on your keyboard.

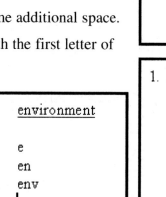

18. Press **<Tab>** to indent your cursor.

19. Type the first and second letters of the spelling word, such as *e* and *n*, and press **<Enter>** or **<Return>** on your keyboard.

20. Press **<Tab>** to indent your cursor.

21. Type the first, second, and third letters of the spelling word, such as *e*, *n*, and *v*, and press **<Enter>** or **<Return>** on your keyboard.

22. Continue in this manner until the entire spelling word is typed.

23. To place a right triangle around the spelling triangle you just typed, click on the **AUTOSHAPES** menu button on the **Drawing Toolbar**, pull up to *Basic Shapes*, and then select the **Right Triangle.**

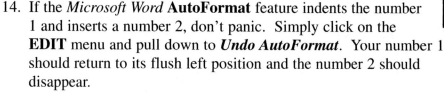

Super Spelling Triangles *(cont.)*

Introducing the Project *(cont.)*

Special Note: If you don't see the **AutoShapes** button below your horizontal scroll bar, click on the **VIEW** menu, pull down to *Toolbars*, and then select **Drawing**. The **Drawing Toolbar** with the **AutoShapes** button should now appear below your horizontal scroll bar.

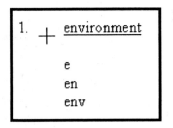

24. After selecting the **Right Triangle,** your cursor will turn into a crosshair. Place the crosshair above and to the left of the first letter of your spelling word, such as *e*. Click and drag down and to the right. Release the mouse button when you have created a triangle. (Notice that the crosshair turns into an insertion point when you hold down the mouse button.)

25. Don't worry if your clicking and dragging is not perfect. Resizing the triangle is easy. If you wish to make the triangle taller, move your cursor over the upper-left resizing button. When the cursor changes to a double-headed resizing arrow, click and drag upward. Notice that the cursor changes to a crosshair when you click and hold down the mouse button. Release the mouse button when the triangle is the size you desire.

26. You can also resize from the bottom, if the triangle is too long. Move your cursor over the middle-bottom resizing button. When the cursor changes to a double-headed resizing arrow, click and drag upward.

27. When you are done resizing the triangle, format it so that it is displayed behind the text rather than on top of the text. Right-click (Windows) or push control and click (Mac) on the triangle. A pop-up menu will appear.

28. Click on **Format AutoShape**.

    Special Note: For *Word 97/98* users, click on **Order** and pull down to **Send Behind Text**.

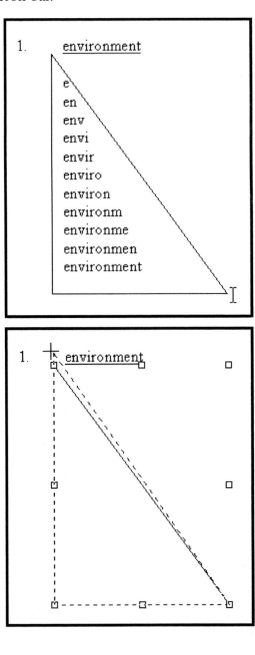

Super Spelling Triangles *(cont.)*

29. At the **Format AutoShape** window, click on the **Layout** (or **Wrapping**) tab to bring it to the forefront.

30. Under **Wrapping style**, click on the **Behind text** button, and then click **OK**.

31. When you return to your document, click away from the triangle to deselect it. You should now see your spelling text within the right triangle.

32. If you need to adjust (move) the triangle, click on it once again to select it. Use the arrow keys on your keyboard to nudge the triangle into place. When you are finished, click away from the right triangle to deselect it.

33. Click below the completed Spelling Triangle and press **<Enter>** or **<Return>** to leave some space. You are now ready for your second spelling word.

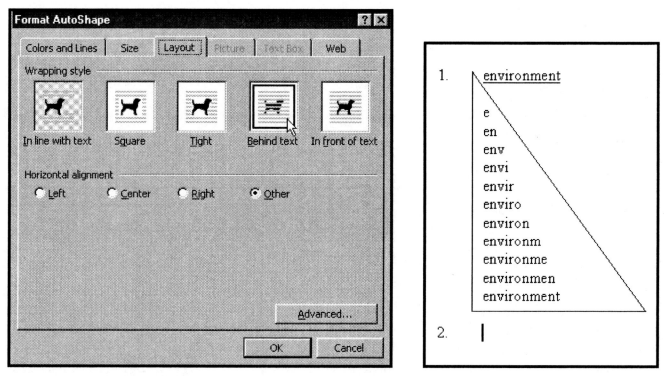

Producing the Project

Once students understand how to make their spelling triangles, allow them to do so. Students can launch *Microsoft Word*, open a new document, and begin on their own. Alternately, you can provide them with the *My Spelling Triangles Template* that is shown on the following page. The *My Spelling Triangles Template* file is also available on the CD-ROM [filename: spelltem.doc]. As you can see, the template file provides students with a preformatted title and a sample spelling triangle.

Presenting the Project

- Have students save and print their spelling triangles. Spelling triangles can also be cut out and displayed on a wall or bulletin board of your classroom.

Super Spelling Triangles *(cont.)*

Additional Project Ideas

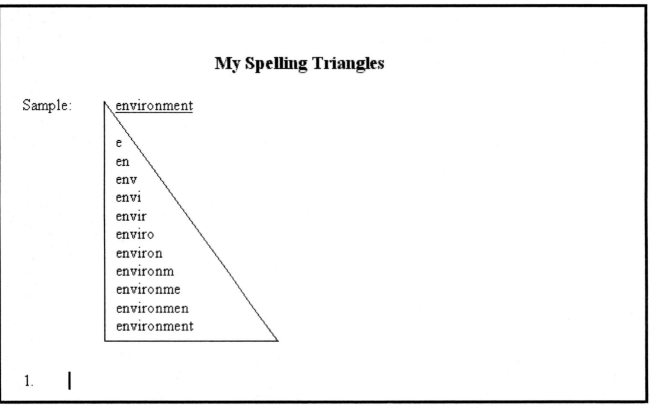

My Spelling Triangles

Sample:

environment

```
e
en
env
envi
envir
enviro
environ
environm
environme
environmen
environment
```

1.

- Have students make vocabulary triangles for words they need to learn in any content area.

- Have students experiment with other shapes found in the *Microsoft Word* **AutoShapes**. For example, have students center their spelling words and list them from the shortest word to the longest word. Place this text within an isosceles triangle as shown on this page. Students can also place their words within a hexagon, placing shorter words at the top and bottom and longer words in the middle of the list.

Additional Resources

- Visit the *Harcourt School Publishers: The Learning Site* Web site. There you will find a series of Spelling Checks and Word Builders for grades 1 through 6. The Spelling Checks help students identify and correct misspelled words. The Word Builders include interactive games where students can click and drag letters to form words and more. The Internet site address is:

http://www.harcourtschool.com/menus/harcourt_brace_spelling.html

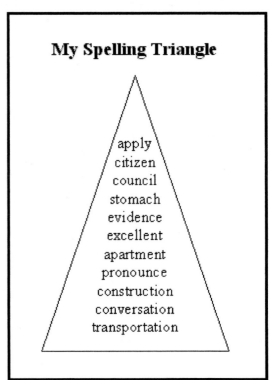

My Spelling Triangle

```
apply
citizen
council
stomach
evidence
excellent
apartment
pronounce
construction
conversation
transportation
```

Making Math Tables

Project Description

In this activity, students make their own multiplication tables in *Microsoft Word*.

X	0	1	2	3	4	5	6	7	8	9	10	11	12
0	0	0	0	0	0	0	0	0	0	0	0	0	0
1	0	1	2	3	4	5	6	7	8	9	10	11	12
2	0	2	4	6	8	10	12	14	16	18	20	22	24
3	0	3	6	9	12	15	18	21	24	27	30	33	36
4	0	4	8	12	16	20	24	28	32	36	40	44	48
5	0	5	10	15	20	25	30	35	40	45	50	55	60
6	0	6	12	18	24	30	36	42	48	54	60	66	72
7	0	7	14	21	28	35	42	49	56	63	70	77	84
8	0	8	16	24	32	40	48	56	64	72	80	88	96
9	0	9	18	27	36	45	54	63	72	81	90	99	108
10	0	10	20	30	40	50	60	70	80	90	100	110	120
11	0	11	22	33	44	55	66	77	88	99	110	121	132
12	0	12	24	36	48	60	72	84	96	108	120	132	144

Hardware and Software Needed

For this activity, you will need your computer system and *Microsoft Word*. You will also want access to a printer.

Materials You Will Need

None.

CD-ROM Files

Name	Description	Filename
Multiplication Table	Resource file	multable.doc
Multiplication Table Template	Multiplication table template	multemp.doc
Addition Table	Resource file	addtable.doc
Addition Table Template	Addition table template	addtemp.doc

Introducing the Project

Review with students some of their multiplication facts. Share with students the sample *Multiplication Table* that is shown on the following page and is available on the CD-ROM [filename: multable.doc].

Demonstrate to students how the *Multiplication Table* can be used to locate the answers to their multiplication problems. Have students select a multiplication problem, such as 4 x 7. Show students how they can find the 4 along the top of the *Multiplication Table* and find the 7 along the left side. Where the two numbers intersect within the table (28) is the answer to their problem.

Have students practice using the *Multiplication Table* until you feel that they have an understanding of how it is used. Then explain to students that they will be creating their own multiplication tables.

X	0	1	2	3	4	5	6	7	8	9	10	11	12
0	0	0	0	0	0	0	0	0	0	0	0	0	0
1	0	1	2	3	4	5	6	7	8	9	10	11	12
2	0	2	4	6	8	10	12	14	16	18	20	22	24
3	0	3	6	9	12	15	18	21	24	27	30	33	36
4	0	4	8	12	16	20	24	28	32	36	40	44	48
5	0	5	10	15	20	25	30	35	40	45	50	55	60
6	0	6	12	18	24	30	36	42	48	54	60	66	72
7	0	7	14	21	28	35	42	49	56	63	70	77	84
8	0	8	16	24	32	40	48	56	64	72	80	88	96
9	0	9	18	27	36	45	54	63	72	81	90	99	108
10	0	10	20	30	40	50	60	70	80	90	100	110	120
11	0	11	22	33	44	55	66	77	88	99	110	121	132
12	0	12	24	36	48	60	72	84	96	108	120	132	144

Making Math Tables *(cont.)*

Multiplication Table

X	0	1	2	3	4	5	6	7	8	9	10	11	12
0	0	0	0	0	0	0	0	0	0	0	0	0	0
1	0	1	2	3	4	5	6	7	8	9	10	11	12
2	0	2	4	6	8	10	12	14	16	18	20	22	24
3	0	3	6	9	12	15	18	21	24	27	30	33	36
4	0	4	8	12	16	20	24	28	32	36	40	44	48
5	0	5	10	15	20	25	30	35	40	45	50	55	60
6	0	6	12	18	24	30	36	42	48	54	60	66	72
7	0	7	14	21	28	35	42	49	56	63	70	77	84
8	0	8	16	24	32	40	48	56	64	72	80	88	96
9	0	9	18	27	36	45	54	63	72	81	90	99	108
10	0	10	20	30	40	50	60	70	80	90	100	110	120
11	0	11	22	33	44	55	66	77	88	99	110	121	132
12	0	12	24	36	48	60	72	84	96	108	120	132	144

Making Math Tables *(cont.)*

Multiplication Table by _____

X	0	1	2	3	4	5	6	7	8	9	10	11	12
0													
1													
2													
3													
4													
5													
6													
7													
8													
9													
10													
11													
12													

Making Math Tables *(cont.)*

Producing the Project

Using the *Multiplication Table Template* that is shown on the previous page, help students to systematically fill in the table. The *Multiplication Table Template* is also available on the CD-ROM [filename: multemp.doc].

First, have students multiply by zero and fill in the 0s column as shown below. Then have students multiply by one and fill in the 1s column. Continue in this manner until students have filled in the entire table.

X	0	1	2	3	4	5	6	7	8	9	10	11	12
0	0												
1	0												
2	0												
3	0												
4	0												
5	0												
6	0												
7	0												
8	0												
9	0												
10	0												
11	0												
12	0												

X	0	1	2	3	4	5	6	7	8	9	10	11	12
0	0	0											
1	0	1											
2	0	2											
3	0	3											
4	0	4											
5	0	5											
6	0	6											
7	0	7											
8	0	8											
9	0	9											
10	0	10											
11	0	11											
12	0	12											

Presenting the Project

- Have students tape their multiplication tables to their desktops or place them into their notebooks for quick reference.

Additional Project Ideas

- Have students make an *Addition Table* following the same design as the *Multiplication Table*. An *Addition Table* sample is shown to the right and is available on the CD-ROM [filename: addtable.doc]. An *Addition Table Template* is shown on the following page. It is also available on the CD-ROM [filename: addtemp.doc].

+	0	1	2	3	4	5	6	7	8	9	10
0	0	1	2	3	4	5	6	7	8	9	10
1	1	2	3	4	5	6	7	8	9	10	11
2	2	3	4	5	6	7	8	9	10	11	12
3	3	4	5	6	7	8	9	10	11	12	13
4	4	5	6	7	8	9	10	11	12	13	14
5	5	6	7	8	9	10	11	12	13	14	15
6	6	7	8	9	10	11	12	13	14	15	16
7	7	8	9	10	11	12	13	14	15	16	17
8	8	9	10	11	12	13	14	15	16	17	18
9	9	10	11	12	13	14	15	16	17	18	19
10	10	11	12	13	14	15	16	17	18	19	20

Making Math Tables *(cont.)*

Additional Resources

- Do your students need help with their multiplication tables? *The Facts—Just Give Me the Facts!* provides you with some wonderful tips for helping your students with multiplication.

  http://www.col-ed.org/cur/math/math02.txt

+	0	1	2	3	4	5	6	7	8	9	10
0											
1											
2											
3											
4											
5											
6											
7											
8											
9											
10											

- Anyone in your class like baseball? Thought so! Visit the *Funbrain.com Math Baseball* Web site. Students can "swing" by solving addition, subtraction, multiplication, or division problems from "easy" to "super-brain" levels. If the answer is correct, they get a "hit." (The game is designed for one or two players.)

  http://www.funbrain.com/math/

- Download *Math Addict*—a free electronic math flashcard program "written to teach people addition, subtraction, multiplication, and division tables."

  http://www.mathaddict.com/

- Let your students try *Funbrain.com Power Football*. In this game, students answer easy, medium, hard, or super-brain addition, subtraction, multiplication, or division problems to move the football closer to the goal. There is also an option for playing "Algebra" style.

  http://www.funbrain.com/football/index.html

- At the *Interactive Multiplication Table* Web site, your students can type in any multiplication problem with factors from 0 to 12 and see how the multiplication table works.

  http://www.aplusmath.com/cgi-bin/hh/mtable

- Students can practice their addition, subtraction, multiplication, and division facts at *Flash!*

  http://www.meganova.com/megakids/flash.htm

Creating Fraction Games

Project Description

In this activity, students create mathematics card games. First, students make equivalent fraction cards in *Microsoft Word*. After printing and cutting out the equivalent fraction cards, students play Equivalent Fraction Concentration. Second, students make fractions and their decimal conversions cards in *Microsoft Word*. After printing and cutting out the fractions and their decimal conversion cards, students play Fraction to Decimal Conversions Concentration.

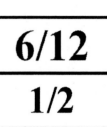

Hardware and Software Needed

For this activity, you will need your computer system and *Microsoft Word*.

Materials You Will Need

For this activity, you will need thick, sturdy paper, such as construction paper or oak tag, for printing the Equivalent Fraction Concentration cards and the Fraction to Decimal Conversions Concentration cards. You may also wish to laminate the cards, so that they last longer.

CD-ROM Files

Name	Description	Filename
Equivalent Fractions Shapes	Resource file	equivshp.doc
Equivalent Fractions Cards Samples	Resource file	eqfracsm.doc
Concentration Cards Template	Template file	conctemp.doc
Fraction to Decimal Conversions Cards	Resource file	fradecc.doc

Introducing the Projects

Project 1—Equivalent Fractions Concentration Game

Review with students the concept of equivalent fractions—two fractions that are equal when written in simplest form. If you choose, share with students the sample *Equivalent Fractions Shapes* that are shown on the following page and are available on the CD-ROM [filename: equivshp.doc]. Discuss with students how 1 whole is equivalent to 2 halves **and** 4 fourths no matter what the shape or form. Covering parts of the shapes, demonstrate how 1 half and 2 fourths are the same as well. Have students make their own equivalent fraction shapes for the fractions you plan to use for the project.

Creating Fraction Games *(cont.)*

Equivalent Fractions Shapes

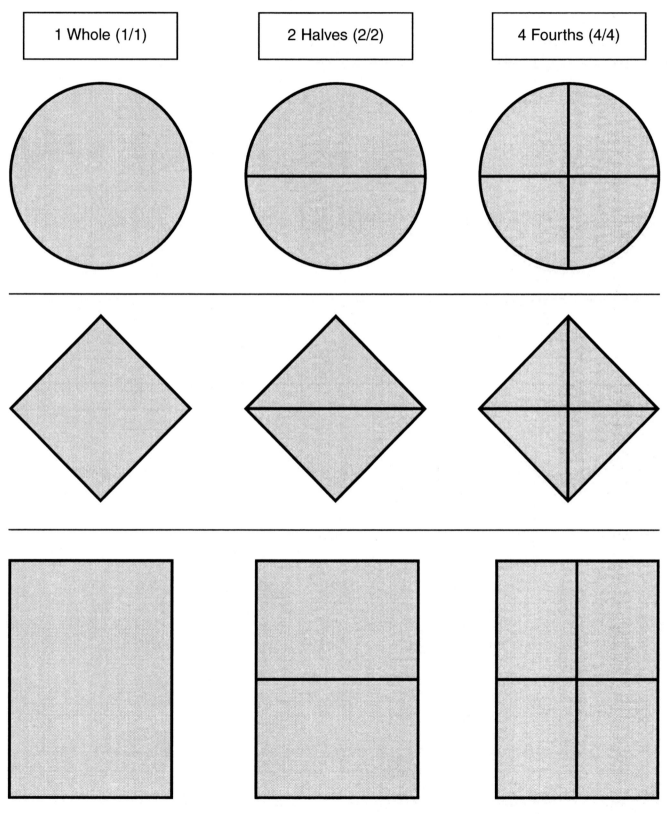

| 1 Whole (1/1) | 2 Halves (2/2) | 4 Fourths (4/4) |

Creating Fraction Games (cont.)

Equivalent Fractions Cards Samples

1/2	1/2	1/2
2/4	3/6	4/8
1/2	1/2	1/2
5/10	6/12	7/14
1/2	1/2	1/2
8/16	9/18	10/20

1/3	1/3	1/3
2/6	3/9	4/12
1/3	1/3	1/4
5/15	6/18	2/8
1/4	1/4	1/4
3/12	4/16	5/20

Creating Fraction Games (cont.)

Fraction to Decimals Conversions Cards Samples

1/1	1/2	1/3
1	0.5	0.3
2/3	1/4	1/5
0.67	0.25	0.2
2/5	3/5	4/5
0.4	0.6	0.8

1/7	2/7	3/7
0.143	0.286	0.429
4/7	5/7	6/7
0.571	0.714	0.857
1/8	3/8	5/8
0.125	0.375	0.625

Creating Fraction Games (cont.)

Introducing the Projects (cont.)

Project 2—Fraction to Decimals Conversions Game

Review with students how to convert fractions to decimals by:

1. dividing the numerator of the fraction by the denominator, and

2. rounding to the precision instructed (so you must determine if you will have students round to the nearest hundredth, thousandth, or ten thousandth place).

Demonstrate this to students with examples, such as 1 divided by 2 equals 0.5.

Producing the Projects

Project 1—Equivalent Fractions Concentration

Brainstorm a list of equivalent fractions that students know, such as ½ = ¾, ½ = ⅜, and so on. Once students have brainstormed a sufficient list for the Equivalent Fractions Concentration Game, they are ready to make their equivalent fraction cards.

Prior to doing so, you may choose to share with students the *Equivalent Fractions Cards Samples* that are shown on page 32. The *Equivalent Fractions Cards Samples* file is also available on the CD-ROM [filename: eqfracsm.doc].

You will find a *Concentration Cards Template* for students to use when they create their own cards on the following page. The *Concentration Cards Template* is also available on the CD-ROM [filename: conctemp.doc].

Once students have entered the equivalent fractions on the cards, have them print the cards and carefully cut them out. If you choose, have students make extra sets that they can take home to play with family members and friends.

Project 2—Fraction to Decimal Conversions Concentration

Brainstorm a list of fraction to decimal conversions that students know, such as ¼ = 1, ½ = 0.5, and so on. Once students have brainstormed a sufficient list for the Fraction to Decimal Conversions Concentration Game, have them enter the fractions and their decimal conversions onto cards.

Prior to doing so, you may choose to share with students the *Fraction to Decimal Conversions Cards Samples* that are shown on page 33. The *Fraction to Decimal Conversions Cards Samples* file is also available on the CD-ROM [filename: fradecc.doc].

You will find a *Concentration Cards Template* for students to use when they create their own cards on the following page. The *Concentration Cards Template* is also available on the CD-ROM [filename: conctemp.doc].

Once students have entered all the fractions and their decimal conversions on the cards, have them print the cards and carefully cut them. If you choose, have students make extra sets that they can take them home to play with family members and friends.

Creating Fraction Games *(cont.)*

Concentration Cards Template

Creating Fraction Games *(cont.)*

Presenting the Projects

Project 1—Equivalent Fractions Concentration

- Now that students have made their Equivalent Fractions Concentration Game, place a set of the game in a learning center or game tote for students to check out. Then let students play away!

- If you have an extra set, place the cards on a wall in your classroom near the entrance. Ask students to find equivalent fractions on their way in and out of the classroom.

Project 2—Fraction to Decimal Conversions Concentration

- Now that students have made their Fraction and Decimal Conversions Concentration Game, place it in a learning center or game tote for check out. Then let students play away!

- If you have an extra set, place the cards on a wall in your classroom near the entrance. Ask students to find a fraction and its decimal conversion on their way in and out of the classroom.

Additional Project Ideas

- Have students make concentration games for other mathematics concepts you are teaching, including any of the following:

  - converting percentages to fractions where students remove the percent sign, make a fraction with the percent as the numerator and 100 as the denominator, and then reduce the fraction if possible. For example:

    $75\% = {}^{75}\!/_{100} = {}^{3}\!/_{4},$
    $48\% = {}^{48}\!/_{100} = {}^{12}\!/_{25},$
    $15\% = {}^{15}\!/_{100} = {}^{3}\!/_{20};$

  - comparing mass in grams, such as:

    1 kilogram = 1000 grams,
    1 hectogram = 100 grams,
    1 dekagram = 10 grams;

  - converting metric volumes, such as:

    1 kiloliter = 1000 liters,
    1 hectoliter = 100 liters,
    1 dekaliter = 10 liters;

  - finding ratios, such as:

    1:5 = 6:30,
    1:25 = 3:75,
    1:3 = 10:30.

Creating Fraction Games *(cont.)*

Additional Resources

- Have your students try the *Funbrain.com—Fresh Baked Fractions* game. In order to play, students are shown four fractions. They have to find the one fraction that is not equivalent. If students answer 24 problems correctly, they become Master Pie Bakers! (Students can choose from easy, medium, hard, and super-brain levels for play.)

  http://www.funbrain.com/fract/index.html

- Visit *Dave's Math Tables: Fraction to Decimal Conversions* to view a table of all the fraction-decimal conversions (in lowest terms) from $\frac{1}{1}$ through $\frac{31}{32}$. This site can become the definitive resource as your students create the Fraction to Decimal Conversions Concentration game.

  http://www.sisweb.com/math/general/arithmetic/fradec.htm

- *All About Decimals* covers decimals operations and includes explanations, interactive practice sessions, and challenge games. The major topic areas are: naming, adding, subtracting, multiplying, dividing, and rounding decimals; place values; comparing decimals; finding percents; equivalent fractions and decimals; and converting. You will really like this site!

  http://www.aaamath.com/dec.html

- *All About Fractions* covers basic fractions, as well as adding, comparing, converting, dividing, multiplying, reducing, and subtracting fractions. There are explanations, interactive practice sessions, and challenge games available for your students at this site.

  http://www.aaamath.com/fra.html

Comparing Native Americans

Project Description

In this activity, students learn about a variety of Native American tribes. Students compare the homes, food, clothing, language, traditional locations, and more of native people, such as the Pueblo and Chinook Indians. Students gather research data in a *Microsoft Word* table and present their findings in a Venn diagram.

Hardware and Software Needed

For this activity, you will need your computer system and *Microsoft Word*. For one of the suggested presentations, you will also need *Microsoft PowerPoint*.

Materials You Will Need

For this activity, it would be helpful if you have a variety of books about Native Americans available in your classroom or reserved for your students to use in the media center.

CD-ROM Files

Name	Description	Filename
A Comparison of Native Americans	Research organizer template	natamtem.doc
A Comparison of Pueblo and Chinook Homes	Research organizer sample	natamsam.doc
Comparing Native Americans Sample	Presentation sample	nampresm.ppt
Comparing Native Americans	Presentation template	nampretm.ppt

Introducing the Project

Discuss with students the different Native American tribes that lived throughout the United States before it was a country. Have students make a list of the native people they are familiar with, such as the Apache, Cherokee, Chinook, Comanche, Iroquois, Ojibwa, Pueblo, Seminole, and Sioux Indians.

Point out to students that not all Native Americans lived the same lifestyle. How the Native Americans lived was determined by their environments (such as the terrain and the climate), their cultures (such as their religious beliefs and social customs), and more.

Then have students make a list of how they can compare the different Native American tribes. Suggestions for comparisons include the following:

- Comparing Native American Homes—
  - Where did they live, and in what types of homes did they live?

Comparing Native Americans (cont.)

- Comparing Native American Foods—

    - How did they obtain food, and what did they eat?

- Comparing Native American Clothing—

    - What types of clothing did they wear, and how was their clothing made?

- Comparing Native American Communication—

    - How did tribes communicate with other Native Americans, and what languages did they speak?

- Comparing Native American Beliefs and Customs—

    - What were their religious beliefs and social customs?

Divide students into small groups of research teams (with two to four students in each). Have each group of students select two Native American people (such as the Apache and the Comanche) and one subject area (such as homes, food, or clothing) to research.

Producing the Project

Provide students with the *A Comparison of Native Americans* research organizer that is shown on the following page and is also available on the CD-ROM [filename: natamtem.doc].

If you choose, share with students the sample completed projects entitled *A Comparison of Pueblo and Chinook Homes* that are shown on pages 43 and 44. The sample research organizer is also available on the CD-ROM [filename: natamsam.doc].

Have students look at their research organizer and the sample research organizer and complete the following:

- On the first page, have students remove the first two underlines in the title and insert the names of the Native Americans they are assigned to research, such as *Pueblo* and *Chinook*.

- On the first page, have students remove the third underline in the title and insert the subject area they are assigned to research, such as *Homes*.

- On the first page, have students remove the two underlines in the first row (the title row) of the table and insert the names of the Native Americans they are assigned to research, such as *Pueblo* and *Chinook*.

- On the first page, have students list five to seven facts about the Native Americans and record their similarities and differences in the Venn diagram on the second page.

- On the first page, have students find and insert pictures that represent some of the facts they found about Native Americans. (The pictures can also be used in the Venn diagram on the second page.)

Comparing Native Americans *(cont.)*

A Comparison of _____ and _____ _____

Directions: Fill in the names of the Native Americans you are comparing in the title above and the column headings below. Fill in the subject of your research in the title above (such as Homes, Food, Clothing, Language, and more). Gather information about the two Native American cultures in your subject area and list what you find in the table below. Find related pictures and place them on this page below the table. When you are finished, create a Venn diagram using the information and pictures you have gathered.

The _____ Indians	The _____ Indians

Directions: Copy and paste the pictures you gathered into the Venn diagram below. Resize and move them so there is room for your text. Place the text information you gathered in the Venn diagram by using text boxes. Resize and move the text boxes as well.

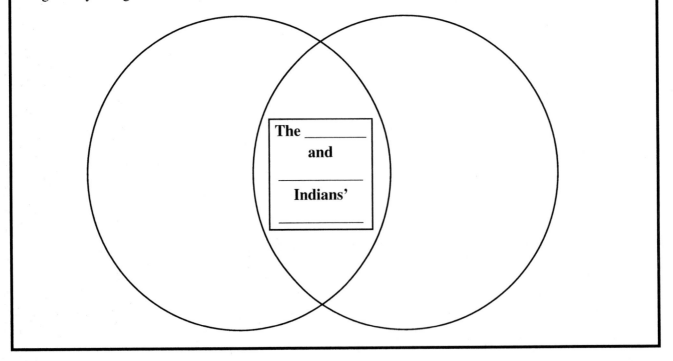

Comparing Native Americans *(cont.)*

Producing the Project *(cont.)*

- Pictures can be inserted by clicking on the **INSERT** menu, pulling down to *Picture*, and then over to *Clip Art*. Students can navigate through the categories provided in the **Insert Clip** window or students can type a key word, such as *Pueblo*, into the **Search for clips** command line. If the desired pictures are not available, allow students to click on the **Clips Online** button that will take them to the *Microsoft Design Gallery* to find and download related pictures.

- On the second page, have students change the title in the center of the Venn diagram to reflect their particular research.

- On the second page, have students copy and paste selected pictures from the first page into the Venn diagram, resizing and moving the pictures so that there is sufficient room for text.

- On the second page, if students insert maps, encourage them to insert arrows to indicate where the Native Americans lived. Students can insert arrows by clicking on the **Arrow** button on the **Drawing Toolbar**, drawing the arrows by clicking and dragging on the Venn diagram, rotating the arrows by clicking on the **DRAW** menu and pulling up to *Rotate* or *Flip* and then selecting the option that will point their arrows properly, and resizing and moving the arrows into their desired positions.

- On the second page, have students insert text boxes and type the text they wish to be displayed in the Venn diagram. Students insert text boxes by clicking on the **Text Box** button on the **Drawing Toolbar**, drawing the text boxes by clicking and dragging on the Venn diagram, inserting the text within the boxes, and resizing and moving the text boxes into their desired positions.

Special Note: If the **Arrow** button, the **Drawing** pop-up menu, or the **Text Box** button is not showing above the **Status Bar**, students should click on the **VIEW** menu, pull down to *Toolbars*, and then select **Drawing**.

Once students have a clear understanding of their assignments, allow them to research their Native Americans. Provide them with an opportunity to use the computer system(s) in your classroom or the lab to input their findings and complete their Venn diagrams.

Presenting the Project

- Once students have completed their *A Comparison of Native Americans* research organizers, have them print the second pages to present to the class. Allow one or two students from each group to explain their Venn diagrams, focusing on the similarities and differences between the two Native American tribes.

- Display the completed Venn diagrams on a bulletin board or wall of your classroom for all to view.

Additional Project Ideas

- Compile your students' Venn diagrams into a *Microsoft PowerPoint* presentation entitled Comparing Native Americans. Three slides from a sample *Comparing Native Americans Sample* presentation file are shown on the following page—the title page, a table of contents page, and a Venn diagram page. The *Comparing Native Americans Sample* presentation file is also available on the CD-ROM [filename: nampresm.ppt].

Comparing Native Americans *(cont.)*

Additional Project Ideas *(cont.)*

- There is also a *Comparing Native Americans* presentation template for you to use with your students. It is available on the CD-ROM [filename: nampretm.ppt]. Simply open the template file and insert your class name on the title slide. Change the table of contents slide to reflect the research activities your students completed. Insert additional table of contents slides with a variety of Native American clip art as necessary. Delete the placeholder on the Venn diagram slide. Have your students select and copy their Venn diagrams with all of their elements (pictures and text) from *Microsoft Word*. Then have students paste the Venn diagrams with all of their elements into *Microsoft PowerPoint*. (Students can select multiple objects by holding down the **<Shift>** key on their keyboards as they click each element.) Add one Venn diagram slide for each group of students who completed their research.

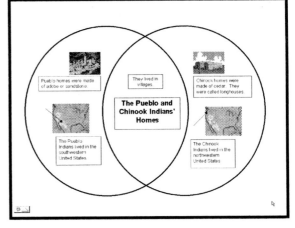

- Have students create their own rock art (on crumpled brown paper) using Native American images. A complete lesson plan for this activity, including pictograph images, is available at *Pages Out of the Past:*

 http://comnett.net/~kolson/Lesson%20Plan.html

- If you, your art teacher, or the school district has a kiln available, have your students make their own Pueblo pottery. You will find a complete step-by-step guide for how to make Pueblo pottery at the *How Pueblo Pottery Is Made* Web site at:

 http://www.collectorsguide.com/fa/fa024.shtml

Additional Resources

- Visit the *Indian Pueblo Cultural Center* to learn about the nineteen Pueblo communities that still exist today.

 http://www.indianpueblo.org/

Comparing Native Americans (cont.)

- Learn more about the Pueblo and other Indians at an *Apache, Pueblo, Zuni Indians* Web site:

http://inkido.indiana.edu/w310work/romac/indians.htm

A Comparison Pueblo and Chinook Homes

Directions: Fill in the names of the Native Americans you are comparing in the title above and the column headings below. Fill in the subject of your research in the title above (such as Homes, Food, Clothing, Language, and more). Gather information about the two Native American cultures in your subject area and list what you find in the table below. Find related pictures and place them on this page below the table. When you are finished, create a Venn diagram using the information and pictures you have gathered on the following page.

The Pueblo Indians	The Chinook Indians
They lived in the southwestern part of the United States (Colorado, New Mexico, Arizona, and Utah areas with some in Texas too).	They lived in the northwestern part of the United States (Washington and Oregon areas).
They lived in villages.	They lived in villages.
Their homes were box shaped.	Their homes were rectangle shaped.
Their homes were built into cliffs or on the desert floor.	Their homes were called longhouses.
Their homes were built of adobe or sandstone.	Their homes were made out of cedar boards.

  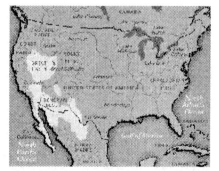

Comparing Native Americans *(cont.)*

Directions: Copy and paste the pictures you gathered into the Venn diagram below. Resize and move them so there is room for your text. Place the text information you gathered in the Venn diagram by using text boxes. Resize and move the text boxes as well.

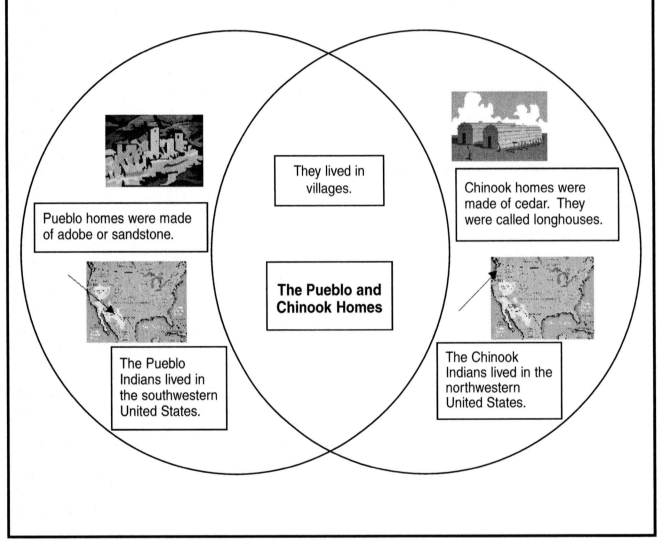

Pueblo homes were made of adobe or sandstone.

They lived in villages.

Chinook homes were made of cedar. They were called longhouses.

The Pueblo and Chinook Homes

The Pueblo Indians lived in the southwestern United States.

The Chinook Indians lived in the northwestern United States.

Collecting Histories Through Timelines

Project Description

In this activity, students learn about timelines through four timeline projects. Have students complete one timeline project or all four of them! First, students create a personal timeline, chronicling their lives from birth to present. Second, students create a timeline for another family member, such as a parent, a grandparent, or a great-grandparent. Third, students create a timeline for a famous person, such as a president, an explorer, a writer, or an artist. Fourth, as a class, students create a timeline of inventions. Their inventions timeline includes hyperlinks to student-written documents that provide additional information about each invention.

Hardware and Software Needed

For this activity, you will need your computer system and *Microsoft Word.*

Materials You Will Need

For this activity, you will need to have a collection of invention books available to your students either in the classroom or reserved in the media center.

CD-ROM Files

Name	Description	Filename
My Life Timeline Sample	Sample timeline	tmlnsamp.doc
My Life Timeline Template	Timeline template	tmlntemp.doc
The Life of Someone Special Timeline Template	Timeline template	someone.doc
The Life of a Famous Person Timeline Template	Timeline template	person.doc
Inventions Timeline Sample	Sample timeline	inventsa.doc
Invention Information Sheet Sample	Sample information sheet	invinfos.doc
Invention Information Sheet Template	Information sheet template	invinfot.doc
The Screw Invention Template	Invention template	screw.doc
The Printing Press Invention Template	Invention template	printing.doc
The Shirt Invention Template	Invention template	shirt.doc
The Bottle Cork Invention Template	Invention template	bottlec.doc
The Pencil Invention Template	Invention template	pencil.doc
The Telescope Invention Template	Invention template	telescop.doc
The Thermometer Invention Template	Invention template	thermome.doc
The Merry-Go-Round Invention Template	Invention template	merry-go.do

Collecting Histories Through Timelines (cont.)

Name	Description	Filename
The Calculator Invention Template	Invention template	calculat.doc
The Submarine Invention Template	Invention template	submarin.doc
The Umbrella Invention Template	Invention template	umbrella.doc
The Megaphone Invention Template	Invention template	megaphon.doc
The Pocket Watch Invention Template	Invention template	pocketwa.doc
The Piano Invention Template	Invention template	piano.doc
The Baby Carriage Invention Template	Invention template	babycarr.doc
The Lightening Rod Invention Template	Invention template	lighteni.doc
The Sextant Invention Template	Invention template	sextant.doc
Bifocal Eyeglasses Invention Template	Invention template	bifocale.doc
The Ambulance Invention Template	Invention template	ambulanc.doc
The Cotton Gin Invention Template	Invention template	cottongi.doc
The Battery Invention Template	Invention template	battery.doc
The Gas Stove Invention Template	Invention template	gasstove.doc
Canned Food Invention Template	Invention template	cannedfo.doc
The Sewing Machine Invention Template	Invention template	sewingma.doc
The Lawnmower Invention Template	Invention template	lawnmowe.doc
The Bicycle Invention Template	Invention template	bicycle.doc
Anesthetics Invention Template	Invention template	anesthet.doc
The Saxophone Invention Template	Invention template	saxophon.doc
The Can Opener Invention Template	Invention template	canopene.doc
The Automobile Invention Template	Invention template	automobi.doc
The Zipper Invention Template	Invention template	zipper.doc
The Bulldozer Invention Template	Invention template	bulldoze.doc
Color Television Invention Template	Invention template	colortel.doc
The Helicopter Invention Template	Invention template	helicopt.doc
The Computer Invention Template	Invention template	computer.doc
Inventions Timeline Template	Timeline template	inventte.doc
Our School Year Timeline Template	Timeline template	timsch.doc

Introducing the Projects

Discuss with students the concept of creating a timeline that shows events over time. Explain to students that there are many types of timelines, such as personal, product, and historical timelines, that can be produced in a variety of ways, such a vertically, horizontally, within tables, with hyperlinks, and more. If you choose, bookmark several of the Internet sites listed in the *Additional Resources* section of this activity to display to students as samples of timelines. **Special Note:** To get to the links quickly, without having to type in the URLs, open the Additional Resources file on the CD-ROM which contains hyperlinks to all of the *Additional Resources* Web sites [filename: addrsorc.doc].

Project 1—My Life Timeline

Share with students the *My Life Timeline Sample*. The first page of the *My Life Timeline Sample* is shown on the following page. The *My Life Timeline Sample* is available in its entirety on the CD-ROM [filename: tmlnsamp.doc]. Discuss with students how Michael gathered information about his life and entered it into the timeline.

Collecting Histories Through Timelines *(cont.)*

My Life Timeline

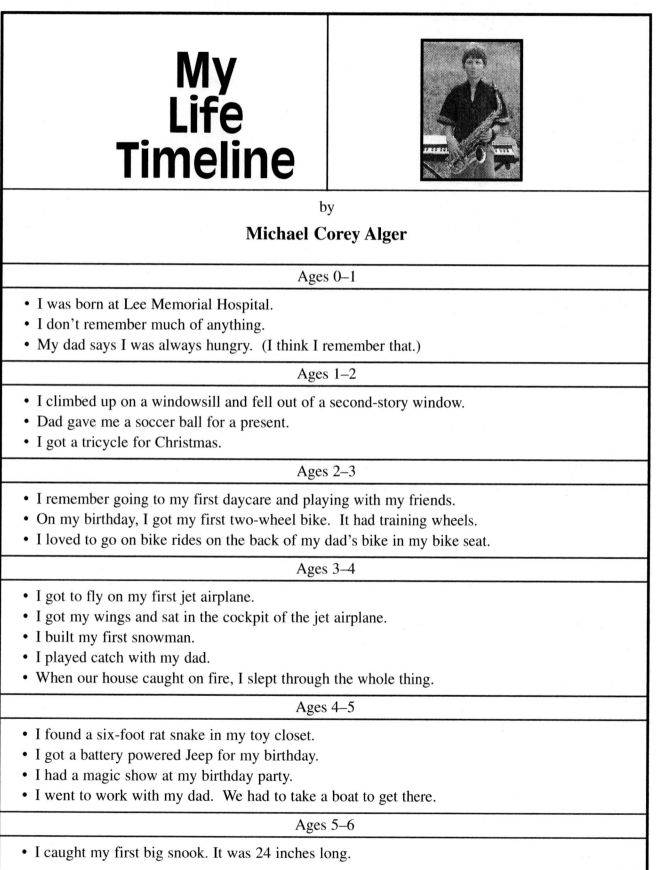

by

Michael Corey Alger

Ages 0–1

- I was born at Lee Memorial Hospital.
- I don't remember much of anything.
- My dad says I was always hungry. (I think I remember that.)

Ages 1–2

- I climbed up on a windowsill and fell out of a second-story window.
- Dad gave me a soccer ball for a present.
- I got a tricycle for Christmas.

Ages 2–3

- I remember going to my first daycare and playing with my friends.
- On my birthday, I got my first two-wheel bike. It had training wheels.
- I loved to go on bike rides on the back of my dad's bike in my bike seat.

Ages 3–4

- I got to fly on my first jet airplane.
- I got my wings and sat in the cockpit of the jet airplane.
- I built my first snowman.
- I played catch with my dad.
- When our house caught on fire, I slept through the whole thing.

Ages 4–5

- I found a six-foot rat snake in my toy closet.
- I got a battery powered Jeep for my birthday.
- I had a magic show at my birthday party.
- I went to work with my dad. We had to take a boat to get there.

Ages 5–6

- I caught my first big snook. It was 24 inches long.

Collecting Histories Through Timelines *(cont.)*

Introducing the Projects *(cont.)*

Project 2—Gathering Family Histories—The Life of Someone Special Timeline

Help students brainstorm a list of family members about whom they can create life timelines. Include grandparents, parents, siblings, and other people that may be "family" to your students. This provides a great opportunity to discuss family relationships, the extended family, and the importance of collecting family histories.

Once the brainstorming is complete, assign or have each student select the person he or she will use for *The Life of Someone Special Timeline.*

Project 3—The Life of a Famous Person Timeline

Help students brainstorm a list of famous people about whom they can create life timelines. Include the presidents, explorers, historical figures, or other groups of people closely related to your curriculum.

Share with students a sample famous-person timeline. Students can learn about the life of our sixteenth president at the *Abe Lincoln Timeline* and view how this timeline was designed. View this timeline at:

http://www.chenowith.k12.or.us/tech/cgcc/projects/bright/lincoln01.htm

Once the brainstorming is complete, assign or have each student select the famous person he or she will use for *The Life of a Famous Person Timeline.*

Project 4—An Inventions Timeline

Explain to students that they will be creating a timeline of inventions. If you choose, share with students the *History of Inventions Timeline* that ranges from 7900 B.C. to 1995 A.D. View this timeline at:

http://www.cbc.ca/kids/general/the-lab/history-of-invention/default.html

Provide students with an opportunity to research inventions, to brainstorm a list of inventions, and to select the inventions they would like to include in their class inventions timeline.

Producing the Projects

Project 1—My Life Timeline

Provide students with a copy of the *My Life Timeline Template* file that is shown on the following page and is also available on the CD-ROM [filename: tmlntemp.doc]. Determine how many bulleted items you would like students to include at each age range. Then direct students to gather information for their personal timelines.

Special Note: The *My Life Timeline Template* file includes age ranges from Ages 0–1 through Ages 12–13. If your students are younger than 13, delete the rows that they do not need.

Collecting Histories Through Timelines (cont.)

My Life Timeline

by

Ages 0–1
-

Ages 1–2
-

Ages 2–3
-

Ages 3–4
-

Ages 4–5
-

Ages 5–6
-

Ages 6–7
-

Ages 7–8
-

Ages 8–9
-

Ages 9–10
-

Ages 10–11
-

Ages 11–12
-

Ages 12–13
-

Collecting Histories Through Timelines *(cont.)*

Producing the Projects *(cont.)*

Project 1 *(cont.)*

- Here's how to delete extra rows. Open the *My Life Timeline Template* file. Click in any cell in the row that you would like to delete or select a range of cells by highlighting them. Click on the **TABLE** menu, pull down to *Delete*, and then select **Rows**. The rows you designated for deletion should disappear from the table.

Once students have gathered their personal timeline data, allow them to enter the information into the *My Life Timeline Template* file. Have students complete the following:

- Open the *My Life Timeline Template* file.

- Before entering any data, click on the **FILE** menu and pull down to *Save As*. (This way, the template file will remain intact.)

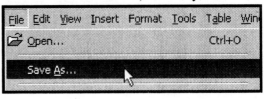

- Navigate to the folder where you have been told to save your file.

- Change the filename to *Life Timeline* with your name at the end, such as *Life Timeline–Michael Corey Alger.*

- Then click on the **Save** button.

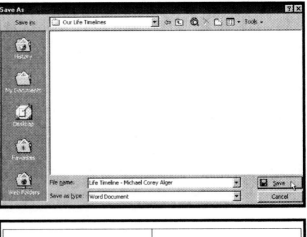

- Now that you have saved the *My Life Timeline Template* file as your very own, you can modify it and enter data. First, modify the file to include your name. Type your name in the line below by to indicate that the *My Life Timeline* was written by you.

- Click after the bullet in the cell below Ages 0–1 and type one memorable event in your life during that time.

- Press **<Enter>** or **<Return>** on your keyboard to move to the next line. A bullet will automatically appear. Type a second memorable event in your life during that time.

- Continue in this manner until you are ready to move to the next age range. Then use the **<Tab>** key on your keyboard, the arrow keys on your keyboard, or simply click after the bullet in the cell below Ages 1–2 and type one memorable event in your life during that time.

Collecting Histories Through Timelines *(cont.)*

- Press **<Enter>** or **<Return>** on your keyboard to move to the next line. A bullet will automatically appear. Type a second memorable event in your life during that time.

- Continue in this manner until you are ready to move to the next age range. Then use the **<Tab>** key on your keyboard, the arrow keys on your keyboard, or simply click after the bullet in the cell below Ages 2–3 and type one memorable event in your life during that time.

- Continuing filling out your timeline. Be sure to save your work from time to time while typing and then again when you are finished. To save your file, click on the **Save** button on the **Standard Toolbar**.

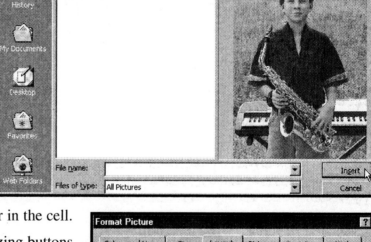

There are several options for including an illustration—a picture, a drawing, or clip art—to the right of the *My Life Timeline* title. Select one option or allow your students to choose which one they would prefer.

If you choose to insert a picture, here's how:

- Click in the cell to the right of the title.

- Click on the **INSERT** menu on the **Standard Toolbar**, pull down to *Picture,* and then over to *From File*.

- At the **Insert Picture** window, navigate to where you saved the picture file, select it, and then click **Insert**. The picture will appear in the cell.

- Click on the picture and use the resizing buttons to make it an appropriate size for the cell.

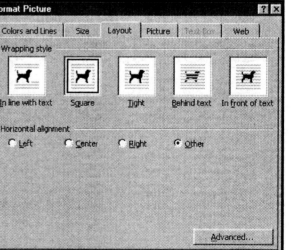

- On Windows machines, right-click your mouse to get a pop-up menu and select **Format Picture**.

- On Macintosh machines, click on the **FORMAT** menu and pull down to *Picture*.

- At the **Format Picture** window, click on the **Layout** (or **Wrapping**) tab to bring it to the forefront if it is not already there.

- Under **Wrapping style**, click on **Square**. Then click **OK** to return to your picture.

Collecting Histories Through Timelines *(cont.)*

Producing the Projects *(cont.)*

Project 1 *(cont.)*

Format Tools Table Window

- Now you should be able to move your picture around in the cell, centering it as best you can.

- To add a border around your picture, click on it once to select it.

- Click on the **FORMAT** menu and pull down to *Borders and Shading.*

- At the **Format Picture** window, click on the **Colors and Lines** tab if it is not already at the forefront.

- Under **Line**, click on the **Color** drop-down menu.

- Select **Black** or another color you would like to use for the border.

- Then change the **Weight** (thickness) of the line from its default setting of **.75 pt** to **3 pt.**

- Then click **OK**.

- When you return to your picture, adjust its position within the cell if necessary. You can add additional space around your picture by clicking in the title cell and adding lines before or after the title. You can add a line before the title by clicking in front of *My* and pressing **<Enter>** or **<Return>** on your keyboard. You can add a line after the title by clicking after *Timeline* and pressing **<Enter>** or **<Return>** on your keyboard.

- Don't forget to **Save** your work!

Collecting Histories Through Timelines (cont.)

If you choose to insert a drawing, here's how:

- Click in the cell to the right of the title.

- Click on the **INSERT** menu on the **Standard Toolbar**, pull down to *Picture*, and over to *From File*.

- At the **Insert Picture** window, navigate to where you saved the drawing, select it, and then click **Insert**. The drawing will appear in the cell.

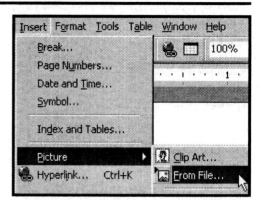

- Click on the drawing and use the resizing buttons to make it an appropriate size for the cell.

- You may wish to center the drawing in the cell by clicking on the **Center** button on the **Formatting Toolbar**.

- To add a border around the drawing, click on it once to select it.

- Click on the **FORMAT** menu and pull down to *Borders and Shading*.

- At the **Borders** window, click on the **Borders** tab to bring it to the forefront if it is not already there.

- Under **Setting:**, select **Box.**

- Click on the **Width** pop-up menu and select **3 pt.**

- Then click **OK.**

- Don't forget to **Save** your work!

Collecting Histories Through Timelines *(cont.)*

Producing the Projects *(cont.)*

Project 1 *(cont.)*

If you choose to insert clip art, here's how:

- Click in the cell to the right of the title.

- Click on the **INSERT** menu, pull down to *Picture*, and then over to **Clip Art**.

- At the **Insert ClipArt** window, navigate until you find a piece of clip art that you like—one that represents you or something about you that is written in the timeline. Then click on the clip art and select the **Insert** button. The clip art will appear in the cell.

- Click on the clip art and use the resizing buttons to make it an appropriate size for the cell.

- On Windows machines, right-click your mouse to get a pop-up menu and select **Format Picture**.

- On Macintosh machines, click on the **FORMAT** menu and pull down to *Picture*.

- At the **Format Picture** window, click on the **Layout** (or **Wrapping**) tab to bring it to the forefront if it is not already there.

- Under **Wrapping style**, click on **Square**. Then click **OK** to return to your picture.

- Now you should be able to move your clip art around in the cell, centering it as best you can.

- Don't forget to **Save** your work!

Collecting Histories Through Timelines *(cont.)*

Here are two more options for the illustration to the right of the title. First, you can have students complete their timelines, print them, and then draw the illustrations with traditional drawing tools, such as crayons, markers, paint, and more.

Second, if you would rather not have students include an illustration, simply merge the two cells and the title will span the entire top of the timeline.

Here's how:

- Click in the title cell and drag to select both this cell and the illustration cell.

- Once both cells are selected (you should see some highlighting in both cells, although the illustration cell will not be completely highlighted), click on the **TABLE** menu and pull down to *Merge Cells*.

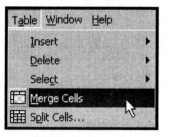

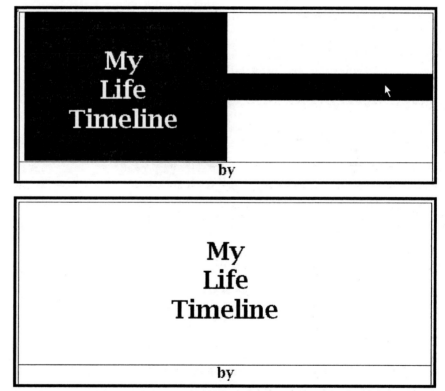

- The title should now appear centered across the top of the *My Life Timeline*.

Project 2—Gathering Family Histories—The Life of Someone Special Timeline

Share with students *The Life of Someone Special Timeline Template* that is shown on page 57 and is available on the CD-ROM [filename: someone.doc].

Collecting Histories Through Timelines *(cont.)*

Producing the Projects *(cont.)*

Project 2 *(cont.)*

Provide students with sufficient opportunity and time to interview or research their special family members. Once students have gathered their special family member data, allow them to enter the information into the *The Life of Someone Special Timeline Template* file. Have students complete the following:

- Open the *The Life of Someone Special Timeline Template* file.

- Before entering any data, click on the **FILE** menu and pull down to *Save As*. (This way, the template file will remain intact.)

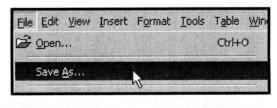

- Navigate to the folder where you have been told to save your file.

- Change the filename to *Someone Special* with your name at the end, such as *Someone Special–Michael Corey Alger*.

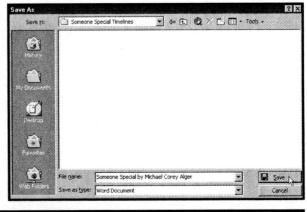

- Then click on the **Save** button.

- Now that you have saved the template file as your very own, you can modify it and enter data. First, enter the name of the special family member. Click and drag over the space holder (the underlining where you will place the person's name) to select (highlight) it.

- Then click on the **Cut** button on the **Standard Toolbar**. The space holder will disappear and your cursor is in position for typing the special family member's name. Type it!

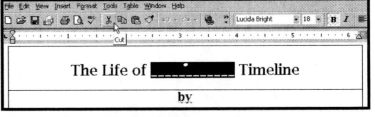

- After typing the special person's name, modify the file to include your name. Type your name in the line below **by** to indicate that the timeline was developed by you.

- Click in the first cell under the **Dates** column heading and enter the date of the first major event in your special family member's life.

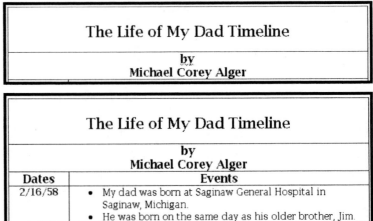

Collecting Histories Through Timelines *(cont.)*

The Life of _____ Timeline	
by	
Dates	**Events**
	•
	•
	•
	•
	•
	•
	•
	•
	•
	•
	•
	•
	•
	•

Collecting Histories Through Timelines *(cont.)*

Producing the Projects *(cont.)*

Project 2 *(cont.)*

- Then click after the bullet in the first cell under the **Events** column heading and enter the details of the first major event in your special family member's life. If more happened on that day, simple press **<Enter>** or **<Return>** on your keyboard to move to the next line. A bullet will automatically appear. Then enter something else about that day.

- To move to the next row, use the **<Tab>** key on your keyboard, the arrow keys on your keyboard, or simply click in the next row with your mouse.

- Continue in this manner until you have completed the timeline for your special family member.

- Be sure to save your work from time to time while typing and then again when you are finished. To save your file, click on the **Save** button on the **Standard Toolbar**.

Project 3—The Life of a Famous Person Timeline

Share with students *The Life of a Famous Person Timeline Template* that is shown on the previous page and is available on the CD-ROM [filename: person.doc].

Provide students with sufficient opportunity and time to interview or research their famous people. Once students have gathered their famous person timeline data, allow them to enter the information into the *The Life of a Famous Person Timeline Template* file. Have students complete the following:

- Open the *The Life of a Famous Person Timeline Template* file.

- Before entering any data, click on the **FILE** menu and pull down to *Save As*. (This way, the template file will remain intact.)

- Navigate to the folder where you have been told to save your file.

- Change the filename to *Famous Person* with your name at the end, such as *Famous Person–Michael Corey Alger.*

- Then click on the **Save** button.

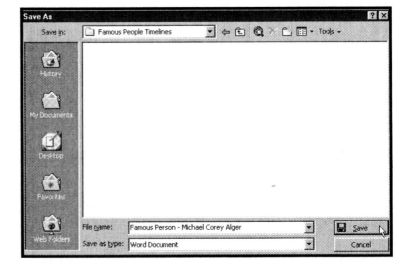

Collecting Histories Through Timelines *(cont.)*

- Now that you have saved the famous person template file as your very own, you can modify it and enter data. First, enter the name of the famous person. Click and drag over the space holder (the underlining where you will place the person's name) to select (highlight) it.

- Then click on the **Cut** button on the **Standard Toolbar**. The space holder will disappear and your cursor is in position for typing the famous person's name. Type it!

- After typing the famous person's name, modify the file to include your name. Type your name in the line below **by** to indicate that the timeline was developed by you.

- Click in the first cell under the **Dates** column heading and enter the date of the first major event in your famous person's life.

- Then click after the bullet in the first cell under the **Events** column heading and enter the details of the first major event in your famous person's life. If more happened on that day, simple press **<Enter>** or **<Return>** on your keyboard to move to the next line. A bullet will automatically appear. Then enter something else about that day.

The Life of Albert Einstein Timeline	
by **Michael Corey Alger**	
Dates	**Events**
/14/1879	• Albert Einstein was born on March 14, 1879, in Ulm, Germany.

- To move to the next row, use the **<Tab>** key on your keyboard, the arrow keys on your keyboard, or simply click in the next row with your mouse.

- Continue in this manner until you have completed the timeline for your famous person.

- Be sure to save your work from time to time while typing and then again when you are finished. To save your file, click on the **Save** button on the **Standard Toolbar**.

Project 4—Inventions Timeline

Share with students the *Inventions Timeline Sample* that is partially shown on this page. The *Inventions Timeline Sample* is available on the CD-ROM [filename: inventsa.doc]. Explain to students that their inventions will be listed in order, according to their dates on the *Inventions Timeline*. Each invention will be linked to its *Invention Information Sheet* that students will be creating.

Inventions Timeline	
by **Mrs. Ray's Class**	
Dates	**Inventions**
1405	• The Screw
1450	• The Printing Press
1500	• The Shirt
1530	• The Bottle Cork
1565	• The Pencil
1590	• The Telescope
1592	• The Thermometer
1620	• The Merry-Go-Round
1623	• The Calculator
1624	• The Submarine
1637	• The Umbrella
1670	• The Megaphone
1675	• The Pocket Watch

Collecting Histories Through Timelines *(cont.)*

Producing the Projects *(cont.)*

Project 4 *(cont.)*

If you are showing the students the *Inventions Timeline Sample* on the your computer system and want to demonstrate how the links work, you will have to copy the *Student Inventions Files* folder (which contains the template files for all the inventions listed) from the CD-ROM onto your desktop, so that it has the same path as when it was developed. Here's how:

- Place the CD-ROM in the CD drive of your computer system.

- Navigate to the CD drive.

- On Windows machines, right-click on the *Student Invention Files* folder and select **Copy**. Then navigate to your **Desktop**. (You can close the CD drive window now.) Finally, right-click on your **Desktop** and select **Paste**.

- On Macintosh machines, click on the *Student Invention Files* folder and drag it from the CD to your desktop.

- The *Student Invention Files* folder should copy onto your **Desktop** within a few seconds.

> **My Invention**
> **The Gas Stove**
> by
> **Sally Student**
>
> | **What** is the invention? |
> | • The invention is the gas stove. |
> | **Who** invented the invention? |
> | • Zachaus Andreas Winzler invented the gas stove. |
> | **When** was the invention invented? |
> | • The gas stove was invented in 1802. |
> | **Where** was invention invented? |
> | • The gas stove was invented in Austria. |
> | **How** was the invention made? |
> | • Zachaus Winzler manufactured the gas fuel and piped it into his home. He used it for cooking. |
> | **Why** is the invention important? |
> | • Now people had an alternative form of fuel for heating their homes and cooking their meals. |

Share with the students the *Invention Information Sheet Sample* that is shown on this page and is available on the CD-ROM [filename: invinfos.doc].

Explain how students will be filling in the "what, who, when, where, how, and why" information about their inventions.

Provide students with the *Invention Information Sheet Template* that is shown on the following page. The *Invention Information Sheet Template* file is available on the CD-ROM [filename: invinfot.doc].

Once students have gathered their invention data, allow them to enter the information into the *Invention Information Sheet Template* file. Have students complete the following:

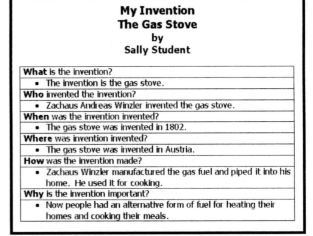

- Open the *Invention Information Sheet Template* file.

- Before entering any data, click on the **FILE** menu and pull down to *Save As*. (This way, the template file will remain intact.)

- Navigate to the folder where you have been told to save your file.

- Change the filename to the name of your invention, such as *The Gas Stove* with your name at the end, such as *The Gas Stove by Sally Student*. Then click on the **Save** button.

Collecting Histories Through Timelines (cont.)

My Invention

_____

by

_____

What is the invention?
•
Who invented the invention?
•
When was the invention invented?
•
Where was invention invented?
•
How was the invention made?
•
Why is the invention important?
•

My Invention

_____

by

_____

What is the invention?
•
Who invented the invention?
•
When was the invention invented?
•
Where was invention invented?
•
How was the invention made?
•
Why is the invention important?
•

Collecting Histories Through Timelines *(cont.)*

Producing the Projects *(cont.)*

Project 4 *(cont.)*

- Now that you have saved the *Invention Information Sheet Template* file as your very own, you can modify it and enter data. First, enter the name of the invention. Click and drag over the space holder (the underlining where you will place the name of the invention) to select (highlight) it.

- Then click on the **Cut** button on the **Standard Toolbar**. The space holder will disappear and your cursor is in position for typing the invention's name. Type it!

- After typing the invention, modify the file to include your name. Click and drag over the space holder for your name to select it.

- Then click on the **Cut** button on the **Standard Toolbar**. The space holder will disappear and your cursor is in position for typing your name. Type it!

- Click after the bullet under **What is the invention?** and type a complete sentence, naming the invention you researched, such as "The invention is the gas stove."

- Then click after the bullet under **Who invented the invention?** and type a complete sentence, naming the person or people who invented the invention, such as "Zachaus Andreas Winzler invented the gas stove."

- Continue in this manner until you have answered all the questions on your *Invention Information Sheet*.

- Be sure to save your work from time to time while typing and then again when you are finished. To save your file, click on the **Save** button on the **Standard Toolbar**.

Special Note: The 35 files in the *Student Invention Files* folder on the CD-ROM (or copied onto your desktop, if you did so) are all template files as well. If your students are researching any of these inventions, feel free to allow them to open these template files and use them. The titles of the inventions are already in place, so students can skip down and begin with entering their names.

Collecting Histories Through Timelines *(cont.)*

Inventions Timeline	
by	
Dates	**Inventions**
	•
	•
	•
	•
	•
	•
	•
	•
	•
	•
	•
	•
	•
	•

Collecting Histories Through Timelines *(cont.)*

Producing the Projects *(cont.)*

Project 4 *(cont.)*

The *Student Inventions Files* folder include: the screw [filename: screw.doc]; the printing press [filename: printing.doc]; the shirt [filename: shirt.doc]; the bottle cork [filename: bottlec.doc]; the pencil [filename: pencil.doc]; the telescope [filename: telescop.doc]; the thermometer [filename: thermome.doc]; the merry-go-round [filename: merry-go.doc]; the calculator [filename: calculat.doc]; the submarine [filename: submarin.doc]; the umbrella [umbrella.doc]; the megaphone [filename: megaphon.doc]; the pocket watch [filename: pocketwa.doc]; the piano [filename: piano.doc]; the baby carriage [filename: babycarr.doc]; the lightening rod [filename: lighteni.doc]; the sextant [filename: sextant.doc]; bifocal eyeglasses [filename: bifocale.doc]; the ambulance [ambulanc.doc]; the cotton gin [cottongi.doc]; the battery [filename: battery.doc]; the gas stove [filename: gasstove.doc]; canned food [filename: cannedfo.doc]; the sewing machine [filename: sewingma.doc]; the lawnmower [filename: lawnmowe.doc]; the bicycle [filename: bicycle.doc]; anesthetics [filename: anesthet.doc]; the saxophone [filename: saxophon.doc]; the can opener [filename: canopene.doc]; the automobile [filename: automobi.doc]; the zipper [filename: zipper.doc]; the bulldozer [filename: bulldoze.doc]; color television [filename: colortel.doc]; the helicopter [filename: helicopt.doc]; and the computer [filename: computer.doc].

Provide students with sufficient opportunity and time to research their inventions.

Once each student has completed his or her *Invention Information Sheet*, it's time to enter the inventions and their dates into the *Inventions Timeline Template* file that is shown on the previous page. The *Inventions Timeline Template* file is available on the CD-ROM [filename: inventte.doc].

- Open the *Inventions Timeline Template* file and type your class name under the **by** line, such as *Mrs. Ray's Class*. Then enter the inventions and their dates in each row.

Once all the inventions are entered, create a hyperlink between each invention and its *Invention Information Sheet*. Here's how:

- Click and drag to select (highlight) one of your student's inventions, such as *The Gas Stove*.

- Then click on the **Insert Hyperlink** button on the **Standard Toolbar**.

- At the **Insert Hyperlink** window, click on the **File** button so that you can navigate to your student's file.

- Select your student's file and then click **OK**.

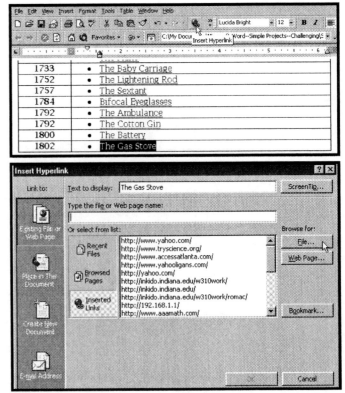

Collecting Histories Through Timelines (cont.)

- When you return to the **Insert Hyperlink** window, simply click **OK** again.

- When you return to your *Inventions Timeline* file, notice that the invention is now blue and underlined. This is an indication that the invention has a hyperlink to another document.

- Move your cursor over the invention and the insertion point will change to a hand. You will also get a pop-up information box that indicates the path to your student's *Invention Information Sheet* about the invention.

- Click on the invention to test the hyperlink. Your student's document should automatically open for your viewing. Close the document when you are finished viewing to return to your *Inventions Timeline*.

Presenting the Projects

Project 1—My Life Timeline

- Display your students' personal timelines on the bulletin board in your classroom or on a wall outside of your classroom.

- Compile your students' personal timelines into a book you could entitle *Our Lives—A Timelines Notebook*. It will be a notebook you will treasure in the years to come.

Project 2—Gathering Family Histories—The Life of Someone Special Timeline

- Have your students orally present their timelines, sharing with their fellow students the names and special events in their family members' lives. Encourage your students to bring pictures of their family members to share during their presentations.

- Make a Special People Classroom Quilt that displays the special family members in your students' lives. Have your students create a variety of quilt patterns on 8.5" by 11" paper. Use one wall of your classroom to piece the quilt patterns together, interspersing the students' timelines throughout.

Project 3—The Life of a Famous Person Timeline

- Display your students' famous people timelines on the bulletin board in your classroom or on a wall outside of your classroom.

- Post the famous person timelines on your classroom Web site to share with the world.

Collecting Histories Through Timelines (cont.)

Presenting the Projects (cont.)

Project 4—Inventions Timeline

- Have students draw illustrations of their inventions on the bottom of their *Inventions Information Sheets*. Display the sheets on the bulletin board in your classroom or on a wall outside of your classroom to share with others.

- Post the *Inventions Timeline* to your classroom Web site to share with others. Be sure to include all of your students' *Invention Information Sheets* when you build the Web page so that visitors to your site can click on any invention and get more information.

Additional Project Ideas

- Host a classroom party for the family members about whom your students created *The Life of Someone Special Timelines*. Have each student introduce his or her guest and tell about two or three events in the special family member's life.

- Have students create a timeline for their school year, noting important events, holidays, and more. You will find a partial *Our School Year Timeline Template* shown below. The entire *Our School Year Timeline Template* is available for you to use on the CD-ROM [filename: timsch.doc]. Feel free to adapt the template to meet your needs. Add rows and delete rows as necessary.

Our School Year Timeline	
by	
Dates	**Events**
August	
	•
	•
	•
September	
	•
	•
	•
October	
	•
	•
	•

- Have students create a timeline for an important historical event that is part of your curriculum, such as the Revolutionary War.

Collecting Histories Through Timelines *(cont.)*

Additional Resources

There are a wide variety of timelines available on the Internet. Here are just a few that demonstrate the range of types and styles of timelines.

- View a *Transportation Technology* timeline from 3500 B.C. (wheeled carts) to 1981 A.D. (first flight of the space shuttle) and everything between at:

   http://www.nationmaster.com/encyclopedia/Timeline-of-transportation-technology

- The colorful *Mexico: Splendor of Thirty Centuries—Timelines* dates from 1000 B.C. to 1521 A.D. View this timeline at:

   http://humanities-interactive.org/splendors.timeline.html

- There is a *Timeline* of the Roman Empire available at:

   http://www.scaruffi.com/politics/romans.html

- A *History Timeline* of the Chinese Dynasties from the Xia Dynasty (2000–2500 B.C.) to The People's Republic of China (1949–present) can be viewed at:

   http://www-chaos.umd.edu/history/time_line.html

- The *Computer Chronicles: From Stone to Silicon* timeline of the history of computing—from the Chinese abacus developed around 3000 B.C. to the popular PCs of today is available at:

   http://library.thinkquest.org/22522/

- It's gold! Learn about *The Great American Gold Rush* at this timeline:

   http://history.sandiego.edu/gen/~jross/goldrush.html

There are lots of books available about inventors and their inventions. Here are just a few:

- *The Smithsonian Visual Timeline of Inventions* by Richard Platt was published by Dorling Kindersley in 1994 [ISBN 1-56458-675-8].

- *Great Inventions* was edited by Richard Wood and published by Time Life Books in 1995 [ISBN 0-7835-4766-8].

- *The Inventor Through History* by Peter Lafferty and Julian Rowe was published by Thomson Learning in 1993 [ISBN 1-56847-013-4].

Science Vocabulary Words
Find 'Em, Match 'Em, and Unscramble 'Em

Project Description

In this activity, students can create three activity sheets to help themselves and others learn science vocabulary words. Have your students make one activity sheet or make all three! First, students create a *Find 'Em* activity sheet, where science vocabulary words are hidden within a word search. Second, students create a *Match 'Em* activity sheet, where science vocabulary words are matched with their definitions. Third, students create an *Unscramble 'Em* activity sheet, where scrambled science vocabulary words are unscrambled and written properly.

Hardware and Software Needed

For this activity, you will need your computer system and *Microsoft Word*.

Materials You Will Need

For this activity, you will need lists of science (or other content area) vocabulary words for students to use when creating the activity sheets.

CD-ROM Files

Name	Description	Filename
The Oceans Vocabulary Words—Find 'Em	Sample activity sheet	ocnfdsa.doc
The Oceans Vocabulary Words—Find 'Em Answer Key	Activity sheet answer key	ocnfdak.doc
The Oceans Vocabulary Words—Match 'Em	Sample activity sheet	ocnmasa.doc
The Oceans Vocabulary Words—Match 'Em Answer Key	Activity sheet answer key	ocnmaak.doc
The Oceans Vocabulary Words— Unscramble 'Em	Sample activity sheet	ocnscsa.doc
The Oceans Vocabulary Words— Unscramble 'Em Answer Key	Activity sheet answer key	ocnscak.doc
Vocabulary Words—Find 'Em Template	Activity sheet template	vocfdtem.doc
Vocabulary Words—Match 'Em Template	Activity sheet template	vocmatem.doc
Vocabulary Words—Unscramble 'Em Template	Activity sheet template	vocsctem.doc

Science Vocabulary Words (cont.)

The Oceans Vocabulary Words—Find 'Em!

Directions: Find the vocabulary words and circle them. Words may be written from the right, from the left, going up, going down, or diagonally.

TECTONICS
ARCHIPELAGO
TIDES
CONTINENTAL SHELF

PLANKTON
TSUNAMI
LAGOON

MOLLUSKS
CRUSTACEANS
ATOLL

Q	W	E	R	T	Y	U	I	O	I	P	L	K	J	H	G
F	D	S	A	Z	X	C	V	M	B	N	M	L	K	J	H
S	G	F	D	S	A	Q	A	W	L	E	R	T	Y	U	I
N	O	P	P	L	K	N	J	H	L	G	F	A	D	S	A
A	Z	L	Z	C	U	V	B	N	O	M	L	R	K	J	O
E	Q	A	W	S	W	E	R	T	T	Y	U	C	I	O	P
C	O	N	T	I	N	E	N	T	A	L	S	H	E	L	F
A	P	K	O	I	U	Y	T	R	E	A	W	I	Q	A	S
T	D	T	F	G	D	J	K	L	M	G	N	P	B	V	C
S	X	O	Z	X	A	E	D	F	G	O	H	E	J	K	L
U	O	N	P	I	U	Y	S	R	E	O	W	L	Q	A	S
R	D	D	F	G	H	Y	J	K	L	N	M	A	N	B	V
C	F	D	S	A	Q	W	E	R	T	Y	U	G	U	I	O
P	L	K	J	H	G	S	K	S	U	L	L	O	M	F	D
X	Z	A	S	V	B	N	M	L	K	O	P	I	U	Y	T
F	R	D	T	E	C	T	O	N	I	C	S	E	W	S	A

Science Vocabulary Words *(cont.)*

The Oceans Vocabulary Words—Match 'Em!

Directions: Draw a line between each vocabulary word and its definition.

Vocabulary Words	Definitions
Tectonics	A great sea wave produced by the earth's movements or volcanic eruptions under water
Archipelago	Invertebrate animals, such as snails and clams, that have a soft body with a hard shell
Tsunami	The edge of a continent that is under the water
Crustaceans	A shallow lake or pond that is near a larger body of water, such as the ocean, but is separated from the larger body
Plankton	The rise and fall of the ocean that is caused by the gravitational pull of the sun and the moon
Mollusks	A coral island consisting of a reef surrounding a lagoon
Tides	The study of the earth's plates and other geological structural features
Continental Shelf	Microscopic animal and plant life in the ocean
Lagoon	Lobsters, shrimp, crabs and other hard-bodied animals that live in the ocean
Atoll	A group of islands

Science Vocabulary Words (cont.)

The Oceans Vocabulary Words—Unscramble 'Em!

Directions: Read the scrambled vocabulary words on the left. Unscramble the vocabulary words and write them correctly on the right.

Scrambled Vocabulary Words	Unscrambled Vocabulary Words
retuccssaan	
knotnalp	
onolag	
loatl	
ttccsenoi	
gapleoihcra	
klumssol	
sited	
flehs altnconitne	
imsuant	

Introducing the Projects

Explain to students that they will be creating some activity sheets in *Microsoft Word* to help themselves and others learn science vocabulary words.

Project 1—Find 'Em!

Share with students *The Oceans Vocabulary Words—Find 'Em* sample activity sheet that is shown on page 69 and is available on the CD-ROM [filename: ocnfdsa.doc]. Explain to students that they will be creating a similar *Find 'Em* activity sheet using the vocabulary words that you provide. If you choose, allow students to complete the activity sheet. *The Oceans Vocabulary Words—Find 'Em Answer Key* is available on the CD-ROM [filename: ocnfdak.doc].

Science Vocabulary Words (cont.)

Project 2—Match 'Em!

Share with students *The Oceans Vocabulary Words—Match 'Em* sample activity sheet that is shown on page 70. *The Oceans Vocabulary Words—Match 'Em* file is available on the CD-ROM [filename: ocnmasa.doc]. Explain to students that they will be creating a similar *Match 'Em* activity sheet using the vocabulary words that you provide. If you choose, allow students to complete the activity sheet. *The Oceans Vocabulary Words—Match 'Em Answer Key* is available on the CD-ROM [filename: ocnmaak.doc].

Project 3—Unscramble 'Em!

Share with students *The Oceans Vocabulary Words—Unscramble 'Em* sample activity sheet that is shown on page 71 and is available on the CD-ROM [filename: ocnscsa.doc]. Explain to students that they will be creating a similar *Unscramble 'Em* activity sheet using the vocabulary words that you provide. If you choose, allow students to complete the activity. *The Oceans Vocabulary Words—Unscramble 'Em Answer Key* is available on the CD-ROM [filename: ocnscak.doc].

Producing the Projects

Provide individual students or small groups of students with the vocabulary words you would like them to use when making the activity sheets. You can even assign vocabulary words for upcoming subject areas, allowing a diversity of activity sheets to be made well ahead of your academic schedule.

Project 1—Find 'Em!

If students are making the *Find 'Em* activity sheet, provide them with the *Vocabulary Words—Find 'Em Template* that is shown on this page. *The Vocabulary Words—Find 'Em Template* file is available on the CD-ROM [filename: vocfdtem.doc].

Direct students to complete the *Find 'Em* activity sheet as follows:

- Remove **<Insert Subject Name>** from the title and insert the subject name, such as The Planets, The Oceans, or The Respiratory System.

- Remove the **<List vocabulary words here.>** spaceholder.

- Type the first vocabulary word.

- Press the **<Tab>** key twice.

- Type the second vocabulary word.

- Press the **<Tab>** key twice.

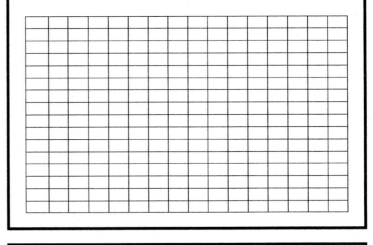

<Insert Subject Name> Vocabulary Words Find 'Em!

Directions: Find the vocabulary words and circle them. Words may be written from the right, from the left, going up, going down, or diagonally.

<List vocabulary words here.>

The Oceans Vocabulary Words

Science Vocabulary Words (cont.)

- Type the third vocabulary word.

- Press the **<Enter>** or **<Return>** key to move to the next line.

- Type the next three vocabulary words, pressing the **<Tab>** key between them so that the vocabulary words align.

- Then press the **<Enter>** or **<Return>** key to move to the next line.

- Continue in this manner until all the vocabulary words are entered.

- Next, enter each vocabulary into the grid. Words can be entered from the right, from the left, going up, going down, or diagonally.

- Double check to make sure all the vocabulary words are entered correctly before going on.

- Carefully enter *phantom* letters in the remaining cells of the grid. Watch closely so that the existing letters for the vocabulary words are not replaced.

- When the entire grid is filled with letters, check to make sure that all the vocabulary words can be found.

- Save the file and print it for others to use while learning their science vocabulary words.

Directions: Find the vocabulary words and circle them. Words may be written from the right, from the left, going up, going down, or diagonally.

TECTONICS	PLANKTON	MOLLUSKS
ARCHIPELAGO	TSUNAMI	CRUSTACEANS
TIDES	LAGOON	ATOLL
CONTINENTAL SHELF		

							I							
						M								
S					A		L							
N	P			N			L			A				
A	L		U				O			R				
E	A	S					T			C				
C	O	N	T	I	N	E	N	T	A	L	S	H	E	L	F
A	K	I						A		I				
T	T		D					G		P				
S	O			E				O		E				
U	N				S			O		L				
R								N		A				
C										G				
				S	K	S	U	L	L	O	M			
		T	E	C	T	O	N	I	C	S				

Q	W	E	R	T	Y	U	I	O	I	P	L	K	J	H	G
F	D	S	A	Z	X	C	V	M	B	N	M	L	K	J	H
S	G	F	D	S	A	Q	A	W	L	E	R	T	Y	U	I
N	O	P	P	L	K	N	J	H	L	G	F	A	D	S	A
A	Z	L	X	C	U	V	B	N	O	M	L	R	K	J	O
E	Q	A	W	S	W	E	R	T	T	Y	U	C	I	O	P
C	O	N	T	I	N	E	N	T	A	L	S	H	E	L	F
A	P	K	O	I	U	Y	T	R	E	A	W	I	Q	A	S
T	D	T	F	G	D	J	K	L	M	G	N	P	B	V	C
S	X	O	Z	X	A	E	D	F	G	O	H	E	J	K	L
U	O	N	P	I	U	Y	S	R	E	O	W	L	Q	A	S
R	D	D	F	G	H	Y	J	K	L	N	M	A	N	B	V
C	F	D	S	A	Q	W	E	R	T	Y	U	G	U	I	O
P	L	K	J	H	G	S	K	S	U	L	L	O	M	F	D
X	Z	A	S	V	B	N	M	L	K	O	P	I	U	Y	T
F	R	D	T	E	C	T	O	N	I	C	S	E	W	S	A

Special Note: The grid in the template file is 16 by 16. So, if your students have a longer vocabulary word, you will have to increase the size of the grid. Here's how:

- To add rows, click in any cell.

- Click on the **TABLE** menu, pull down to *Insert*, and then select **Rows Above**. A new row will appear in the grid.

- To add columns, click in any cell.

- Click on the **TABLE** menu, pull down to *Insert*, and the select **Columns to the Right**. A new column will appear in the grid.

Science Vocabulary Words *(cont.)*

Producing the Projects *(cont.)*

Project 1 *(cont.)*

To make an answer key for the *Find 'Em* activity sheet, direct your students to complete the following:

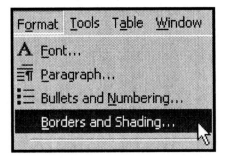

- Save the *Find 'Em* file under a new name that reflects that it is an answer key, such as *Oceans Find 'Em Answer Key*. (If you have character limitations, try the filename: ocnfndak.)

- Highlight one of the vocabulary words, such as *PLANKTON*. (You will not be able to highlight words that are written diagonally. For these, you will have to highlight one letter [cell] at a time.)

- Click on the **TABLE** menu, pull down to *Select*, and then select **Cell**.

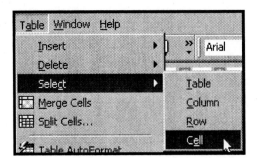

- Click on the **FORMAT** menu and select *Borders and Shading*.

- At the **Borders and Shading** window, click on the **Shading** tab to bring it to the forefront if it is not already there.

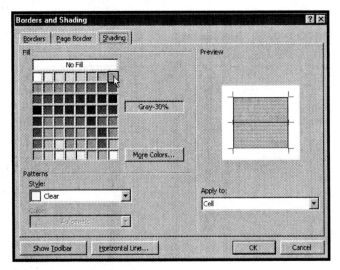

- In the **Fill** area, click on the **Gray-30%** button that is at the end of the first row of grayscale buttons.

- Then click **OK** to return to the grid.

- Continue highlighting words, selecting the cells, and shading them until all of your vocabulary words are shaded.

- Save the answer key and print a copy of it for your teacher.

Science Vocabulary Words *(cont.)*

Project 2—Match 'Em!

If students are making the *Match 'Em* activity sheet, provide them with the *Vocabulary Words—Match 'Em Template* that is shown on this page. The *Vocabulary Words—Match 'Em Template* file is available on the CD-ROM [filename: vocmatem.doc].

Direct students to complete the *Match 'Em* activity sheet as follows:

- Remove **<Insert Subject Name>** from the title and insert the subject name, such as The Planets, The Oceans, or The Respiratory System.

- Enter one vocabulary word in each cell under the **Vocabulary Words** column.

- Enter one definition in each cell under the **Definitions** column. However, don't place the definition directly across from the vocabulary word it defines. Rather, place it in another cell away from the vocabulary word.

- When both columns are filled with vocabulary words and their definitions, check to make sure that they can all be matched correctly.

- Save the file and print it for others to use while learning their science vocabulary words.

Special Note: The template file was designed for ten vocabulary words. If you have fewer vocabulary words or more vocabulary words, you can adjust the template as follows:

- If you wish to delete a row because it is not being used, place your cursor in either the **Vocabulary Words** or **Definitions** cell in that row. Click on the **TABLE** menu, pull down to *Delete*, and then select **Row**. The row will disappear.

<Insert Subject Name> Vocabulary Words

Match 'Em!

Directions: Draw a line between each vocabulary word and its definition.

Vocabulary Words	Definitions

The Oceans Vocabulary Words

Vocabulary Words		Definitions
Tectonics		A great sea wave produced by the earth's movements or volcanic eruptions under water
Archipelago		Invertebrate animals, such as snails and clams, that have a soft body with a hard shell
Tsunami		The edge of a continent that is under the water
Crustaceans		A shallow lake or pond that is near a larger body of water, such

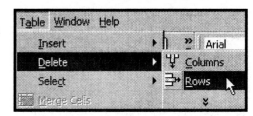

Science Vocabulary Words *(cont.)*

Producing the Projects *(cont.)*

Project 2 *(cont.)*

- If you wish to add another row for an additional vocabulary word, place your cursor in the last **Definitions** cell and press the **<Tab>** key. Another row will appear.

To make an answer key for the *Match 'Em* activity sheet, direct your students to complete the following:

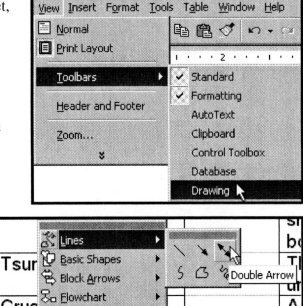

- Save the *Match 'Em* file under a new name that reflects that it is an answer key, such as *Oceans Match 'Em Answer Key.* (If you have character limitations, try the filename: ocnmatak.)

- Draw arrows between the two columns that match each vocabulary word with its definition.

- **Here's How:**

    - Check to see if you have the **Drawing Toolbar** displayed above the **Status Bar**. (If it is not displayed, click on the **VIEW** menu, pull down to *Toolbars*, and then select **Drawing**. The **Drawing Toolbar** should now appear above the **Status Bar** on your screen.)

    - Click on the **AUTOSHAPES** menu on the **Drawing Toolbar**, pull up to *Lines*, and then select **Double Arrow**.

    - Click within a vocabulary word cell, drag the line to the matching definition cell, and drop the line by releasing the mouse button.

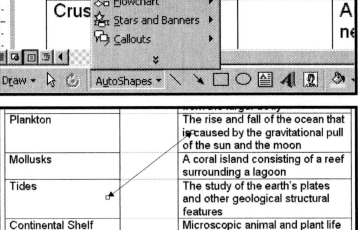

- While the line is still selected (you can tell by the little squares that are at the end of the arrows), you can make it longer or shorter, move the ends of it up and down, and more. When the line is exactly where you want it, click away from it to deselect it.

- Click on the **AUTOSHAPES** menu on the **Drawing Toolbar**, pull up to *Lines*, and then select **Double Arrow**.

- Click within another vocabulary word cell, drag the line to the matching definition cell, and drop the line by releasing the mouse button.

- Continue in this manner until all of the vocabulary words and definitions have lines matching them.

- Save the answer key and print a copy of it for your teacher.

Science Vocabulary Words *(cont.)*

Project 3—Unscramble 'Em!

If students are making the *Unscramble 'Em* activity sheet, provide them with the *Vocabulary Words—Unscramble 'Em Template* that is shown on this page. The *Vocabulary Words—Unscramble 'Em Template* file is available on the CD-ROM [filename: vocsctem.doc].

Direct students to complete the *Unscramble 'Em* activity sheet as follows:

- Remove **<Insert Subject Name>** from the title and insert the subject name, such as The Planets, The Oceans, or The Respiratory System.

- Click in the first blank cell in the **Scrambled Vocabulary Words** column and enter one of the vocabulary words. However, mix up the letters so that the vocabulary word is not spelled right.

- Click in the second blank cell in the **Scrambled Vocabulary Words** column and enter another vocabulary word all mixed up and not spelled right.

- Continue in this manner until you have all the vocabulary words entered under the **Scrambled Vocabulary Words** column.

- Check to make sure that you have entered the unscrambled words correctly. Can you unscramble them?

- Save the file and print it for others to use while learning their science vocabulary words.

<Insert Subject Name> Vocabulary Words

Unscramble 'Em!

Directions: Read the scrambled vocabulary words on the left. Unscramble the vocabulary words and write them correctly on the right.

Scrambled Vocabulary Words	Unscrambled Vocabulary Words

Scrambled Vocabulary Words	Unscrambled Vocabulary Words
retuccssaan	
knotnalp	
onolag	
loatl	
ttccsenoi	
gapleoihcra	
klumssol	
sited	
flehs altnconitne	
imsuant	

Special Note: The template file was designed for ten vocabulary words. If you have fewer vocabulary words or more vocabulary words, you can adjust the template as follows:

- If you wish to delete a row because it is not being used, place your cursor in either the **Scrambled Vocabulary Words** or the **Unscrambled Vocabulary Words** cell in that row. Click on the **TABLE** menu, pull down to *Delete*, and then select **Row**. The row will disappear.

- If you wish to add another row for an additional vocabulary word, place your cursor in the last **Unscrambled Vocabulary Words** cell and press the **<Tab>** key. Another row will appear.

Science Vocabulary Words *(cont.)*

Producing the Projects *(cont.)*

Project 3 *(cont.)*

To make an answer key for the *Unscramble 'Em* activity sheet, direct your students to complete the following:

Scrambled Vocabulary Word	Unscrambled Vocabulary Words
retuccssaan	crustaceans
knotnalp	plankton
onolag	lagoon
loatl	atoll
ttccsenoi	tectonics
gapleoihcra	archipelago
klumssol	mollusks
sited	tides
flehs altnconitne	continental shelf
imsuant	tsunami

- Save the *Unscramble 'Em* file under a new name that reflects that it is an answer key, such as *Oceans Unscramble 'Em Answer Key*. (If you have character limitations, try the filename: *ocnuntak*.)

- Click in the first blank cell in the **Unscrambled Vocabulary Words** column. Across from each scrambled vocabulary word, type the word correctly in this column.

- Continue in this manner until all the vocabulary words are typed correctly in the **Unscrambled Vocabulary Words** column.

- Save the answer key and print a copy of it for your teacher.

Presenting the Projects

- Make copies of the vocabulary word activity sheets that students created. When appropriate, allow the students who created the activity sheets to pass them out to fellow students, collect them, and even grade them.

- Post the activity sheets to your classroom or school Web site, so that students can access them from home to complete and share with their families.

Additional Project Ideas

- The vocabulary word activity sheets are not limited to science. Have students create a variety of them for other subject areas, such as math vocabulary words, health vocabulary words, social studies vocabulary words, and more.

- Have student create a fill-in-the-blank vocabulary activity sheet. Provide students with a list of vocabulary words. Let them write sentences for each word. Then have students remove the vocabulary words from the sentences, leaving blank lines.

Additional Resources

- Visit the *Vocabulary University* Web site. Your students can access free word games and vocabulary puzzles, including definition matching and crosswords. The Internet site address is:

  http://www.vocabulary.com/

- Check out the *Cool Word of the Day* Web site, designed by Merriam Webster to help build your students' vocabulary—one word at a time. So, have students check it daily at:

  http://www.edu.yorku.ca:8080/wotd/

It's "Element"ary!
Learning About the Periodic Table

Project Description

In this activity, students learn about the Periodic Table of the Elements through a series of projects. Have students complete one project or all five of them! In the first project, students are provided with *The Periodic Table* and the *Element Names and Symbols* activity sheets. Students enter the symbol for each element, using the periodic table as their reference guide. In the second project, students are provided with the periodic table with missing elements. Students fill in each missing element based upon its atomic number. In the third project, students are provided with the periodic table with missing atomic numbers. Students fill in each missing atomic number based upon its element. In the fourth project, students research the history of the elements to determine their dates of discovery. In the fifth project, students team up to research element groups or families. Students collect information about the alkali metals, the alkaline earth metals, the transition metals, other metals, metalloids, non-metals, halogens, noble gases, and rare earth elements. Students identify the elements in each group, characteristics of the group elements, and highlight the elements on the periodic table.

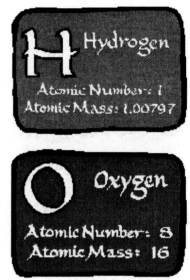

Hardware and Software Needed

For this activity, you will need your computer system and *Microsoft Word*.

Materials You Will Need

For this activity, it would be helpful to have a collection of books about the periodic table and the elements available for your students to use in the classroom or on reserve in the media center. In addition, you may wish to bookmark some of the Internet sites listed in the *Additional Resources* section of this activity for your students to use for their research.

CD-ROM Files

Name	Description	Filename
The Periodic Table	Resource file	pertable.doc
Element Names and Symbols	Activity sheet	names.doc
Element Names and Symbols Answer Key	Answer key	namesans.doc
The Periodic Table—It's "Element"ary	Activity sheet	element.doc
The Periodic Table—Absent Atomic Numbers	Activity sheet	atomic.doc

It's "Element"ary! *(cont.)*

Name	Description	Filename
The Periodic Table—Discovering When the Elements Were Discovered	Activity sheet	discover.doc
Discover Dates Answer Key	Answer key	discovan.doc
Grasping the Element Groups	Activity sheet	grasping.doc
Grasping the Element Groups— Answer Key—Alkali Metals	Answer key	alkali.doc
Grasping the Element Groups— Answer Key—Alkaline Earth Metals	Answer key	alkaline.doc
Grasping the Element Groups— Answer Key—Transition Metals	Answer key	transiti.doc
Grasping the Element Groups— Answer Key—Other Metals	Answer key	othermet.doc
Grasping the Element Groups— Answer Key—Metalloids	Answer key	metalloi.doc
Grasping the Element Groups— Answer Key—Non-Metals	Answer key	nonmetal.doc
Grasping the Element Groups— Answer Key—Halogens	Answer key	halogens.doc
Grasping the Element Groups— Answer Key—Noble Gases	Answer key	noblegas.doc
Grasping the Element Groups— Answer Key—Rare Earth Elements	Answer key	rarearth.doc
The Discovery of Elements Timeline	Sample Timeline	eletime.doc

Introducing the Projects

Share with students *The Periodic Table of the Elements* that is shown on the following page. *The Periodic Table of the Elements* is also available on the CD-ROM [filename: pertable.doc].

Special Note: Authors design and present the periodic table with its element symbols in different ways. For example, sometimes the rows of lanthanide and actinide metals are "pulled out" differently. Also, some of the symbols used for the man-made elements may vary. So, if this version differs in any way from the one you are currently using, feel free to modify the file.

Explain to students that Dmitri Ivanovich Mendeleev first developed the periodic table between 1869 and 1870. He was a chemistry teacher in Russia. At that time, only 57 elements were known.

Mendeleev developed the periodic table to help his students understand the elements. He placed the known elements in the periodic table in atomic number order. Because only 57 elements were known, Mendeleev left lots of blanks in the periodic table. He predicted that scientists would fill in the blanks, and he was right!

It's "Element"ary! *(cont.)*

The Periodic Table of the Elements

Group →

Period	1	2	3	4	5	6	7	8	9	10	11	12	13	14	15	16	17	18
1	H 1																	He 2
2	Li 3	Be 4											B 5	C 6	N 7	O 8	F 9	Ne 10
3	Na 11	Mg 12											Al 13	Si 14	P 15	S 16	Cl 17	Ar 18
4	K 19	Ca 20	Sc 21	Ti 22	V 23	Cr 24	Mn 25	Fe 26	Co 27	Ni 28	Cu 29	Zn 30	Ga 31	Ge 32	As 33	Se 34	Br 35	Kr 36
5	Rb 37	Sr 38	Y 39	Zr 40	Nb 41	Mo 42	Tc 43	Ru 44	Rh 45	Pd 46	Ag 47	Cd 48	In 49	Sn 50	Sb 51	Te 52	I 53	Xe 54
6	Cs 55	Ba 56	*	Hf 72	Ta 73	W 74	Re 75	Os 76	Ir 77	Pt 78	Au 79	Hg 80	Tl 81	Pb 82	Bi 83	Po 84	At 85	Rn 86
7	Fr 87	Ra 88	**	Rf 104	Db 105	Sg 106	Bh 107	Hs 108	Mt 109	Uun 110	Uuu 111	Uub 112						

*	La 57	Ce 58	Pr 59	Nd 60	Pm 61	Sm 62	Eu 63	Gd 64	Tb 65	Dy 66	Ho 67	Er 68	Tm 69	Yb 70	Lu 71
**	Ac 89	Th 90	Pa 91	U 92	Np 93	Pu 94	Am 95	Cm 96	Bk 97	Cf 98	Es 99	Fm 100	Md 101	No 102	Lr 103

* Lanthanide metals
** Actinide metals

Key

Symbol
Atomic Number

It's "Element"ary! *(cont.)*

Introducing the Projects *(cont.)*

Help students read the periodic table. Make sure they understand that the letters represent the symbols for the elements we know about today, and the numbers represent the atomic numbers of the elements.

Explain to students that all elements are made of atoms. The number of protons in the nucleus (center) of an atom of an element determines its atomic number. Hydrogen (H) has only one proton in the nucleus of its atom, so its atomic number is one. Helium (He) has only two protons in the nucleus of its atom, so its atomic number is two. Uranium has ninety-two protons in the nucleus of its atom, so its atomic number is 92. **Special Note:** The atomic number is also sometimes called the proton number.

Producing the Projects

Project 1—Element Names and Symbols

Provide students with a copy of the *Element Names and Symbols* activity sheets. The first page of the activity sheets is shown on the following page. Gradually work through these sheets with students, discussing the elements and helping them enter the symbol for each element listed. The *Element Names and Symbols* activity sheets file is available on the CD-ROM [filename: names.doc]. There is an *Element Names and Symbols Answer Key* also available for you on the CD-ROM [filename: namesans.doc]

Although this activity could also be done off the computer, affording you an opportunity to discuss the elements as students fill in the element symbols, it can also be done on the computer. If you choose to have your students complete this activity on the computer, have them complete the following:

- Open the *Element Names and Symbols* activity sheet.

- Before entering any data, click on the **FILE** menu and pull down to *Save As*. (This way, the activity sheet will remain intact.)

- Navigate to the folder where your teacher has told you to save your file.

- Change the filename to *Element Names and Symbols* with your name at the end, such as *Elements Names and Symbols by Robert B.*

- Then click on the **Save** button.

- Now that you have saved the activity file as your very own, you can enter data.

- Click in the cell to the right of **Hydrogen** and type its symbol—**H**.

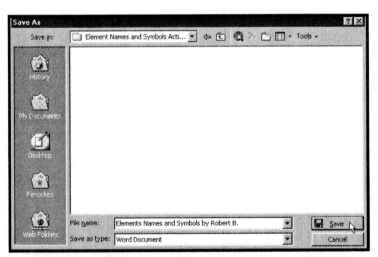

Element Names and Symbols

Directions: Write or type the element symbol for each element. The atomic number has also been listed, so you can use your Periodic Table to help you find them all!

Atomic Number	Element Name	Element Symbol
1	Hydrogen	H
2	Helium	
3	Lithium	

It's "Element"ary! *(cont.)*

Element Names and Symbols

Directions: Write or type the element symbol for each element. The atomic numbers are listed, so you can use your periodic table to help you find them all!

Atomic Number	Element Name	Element Symbol
1	Hydrogen	
2	Helium	
3	Lithium	
4	Beryllium	
5	Boron	
6	Carbon	
7	Nitrogen	
8	Oxygen	
9	Fluorine	
10	Neon	
11	Sodium	
12	Magnesium	
13	Aluminum	
14	Silicon	
15	Phosphorus	
16	Sulfur	
17	Chlorine	
18	Argon	
19	Potassium	
20	Calcium	
21	Scandium	
22	Titanium	
23	Vanadium	
24	Chromium	
25	Manganese	
26	Iron	
27	Cobalt	
28	Nickel	
29	Copper	
30	Zinc	
31	Gallium	
32	Germanium	
33	Arsenic	
34	Selenium	

It's "Element"ary! *(cont.)*

Producing the Projects *(cont.)*

Project 1 *(cont.)*

Special Note: To move from cell to cell, you can click your mouse in the new cell, use the **<Tab>** key on your keyboard to move to the new cell, or use the arrow keys on your keyboard to move to the new cell. Do not press **<Enter>** or **<Return>** on your keyboard. This key only increases the number of lines in your cell. (If you pressed **<Enter>** or **<Return>** by mistake, simply press the **<Backspace>** or **<Delete>** key on your keyboard to remove the extra line(s) in the cell.)

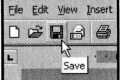

- Then click in the cell to the right of **Helium** and type its symbol—**He**.
- Continue in this manner until you have completed the activity sheet.
- Be sure to save your work from time to time while typing and then again when you are finished. To save your file, click on the **Save** button on the **Standard Toolbar**.

Project 2—The Periodic Table—It's "Element"ary

Provide students with a copy of *The Periodic Table—It's "Element"ary* activity sheet that is shown on the following page. *The Periodic Table—It's "Element"ary* activity sheet is also available on the CD-ROM [filename: element.doc].

Allow pairs of students to work together to fill in the symbols for the missing elements on the computer system in your classroom or in the computer lab. Have students complete the following:

- Open *The Periodic Table—It's "Element"ary* activity sheet.
- Before entering any data, click on the **FILE** menu and pull down to *Save As*. (This way, the activity sheet will remain intact.)
- Navigate to the folder where your teacher has told you to save your file.
- Change the filename to *Elements* with your names at the end, such as *Elements by Reggie and Lorenzo.*
- Then click on the **Save** button.
- Now that you have saved the activity file as your very own, you can enter data.
- Click in the cell above the atomic number **1**. Type **H** for hydrogen.

Period ↓	1	2
1	H 1	
2	3	4

Special Note: To move from cell to cell, you can click your mouse in the new cell, use the **<Tab>** key on your keyboard to move to the new cell, or use the arrow keys on your keyboard to move to the new cell. Do not press **<Enter>** or **<Return>** on your keyboard. This key only increases the number of lines in your cell. (If you pressed **<Enter>** or **<Return>** by mistake, simply press the **<Backspace>** or **<Delete>** key on your keyboard to remove the extra line(s) in the cell.)

- Click in the cell above the atomic number **2**. Type **He** for helium.
- Continue in this manner until your periodic table has all the element symbols.

It's "Element"ary! (cont.)

The Periodic Table
It's "Element"ary

Directions: Fill in the symbol for each element above its atomic number.

← Group →

Period	1	2	3	4	5	6	7	8	9	10	11	12	13	14	15	16	17	18
1	1																	2
2	3	4											5	6	7	8	9	10
3	11	12											13	14	15	16	17	18
4	19	20	21	22	23	24	25	26	27	28	29	30	31	32	33	34	35	36
5	37	38	39	40	41	42	43	44	45	46	47	48	49	50	51	52	53	54
6	55	56	*	72	73	74	75	76	77	78	79	80	81	82	83	84	85	86
7	87	88	**	104	105	106	107	108	109	110	111	112						

*	57	58	59	60	61	62	63	64	65	66	67	68	69	70	71
**	89	90	91	92	93	94	95	96	97	98	99	100	101	102	103

* Lanthanide metals
** Actinide metals

Key

Symbol
Atomic Number

It's "Element"ary! *(cont.)*

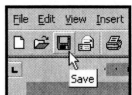

Producing the Projects *(cont.)*

Project 2 *(cont.)*

- Be sure to save your work from time to time while typing and then again when you are finished. To save your file, click on the **Save** button on the **Standard Toolbar**.

Project 3—The Periodic Table—Absent Atomic Numbers

Provide students with a copy of *The Periodic Table—Absent Atomic Numbers* activity sheet that is shown on the following page. *The Periodic Table—Absent Atomic Numbers* activity sheet is available on the CD-ROM [filename: atomic.doc].

Allow pairs of students to work together to fill in the atomic number for each element on the computer system in your classroom or in the computer lab. Have students complete the following:

- Open *The Periodic Table—Absent Atomic Numbers* activity sheet.

- Before entering any data, click on the **FILE** menu and pull down to *Save As*. (This way, the activity sheet will remain intact.)

- Navigate to the folder where your teacher has told you to save your file.

- Change the filename to *Atomic Numbers* with your names at the end, such as *Atomic Numbers by Carletta and Marcella*.

- Then click on the **Save** button.

- Now that you have saved the activity file as your very own, you can enter data.

- Click in the cell below the **H** for hydrogen. Type in the number **1**.

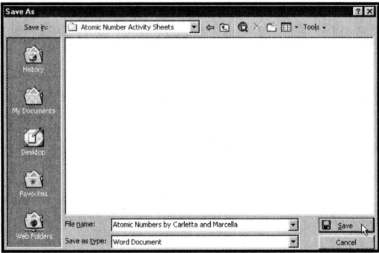

Special Note: To move from cell to cell, you can click your mouse in the new cell, use the **<Tab>** key on your keyboard to move to the new cell, or use the arrow keys on your keyboard to move to the new cell. Do not press **<Enter>** or **<Return>** on your keyboard. This key only increases the number of lines in your cell. (If you pressed **<Enter>** or **<Return>** by mistake, simply press the **<Backspace>** or **<Delete>** key on your keyboard to remove the extra line(s) in the cell.)

- Click in the cell below the **He** for helium. Type in the number **2**.

- Continue in this manner until your periodic table has all the atomic numbers.

- Be sure to save your work from time to time while typing and then again when you are finished. To save your file, click on the **Save** button on the **Standard Toolbar**.

It's "Element"ary! *(cont.)*

The Periodic Table
Absent Atomic Numbers

Directions: Fill in the atomic number below the symbol for each element.

← Group →

Period	1	2	3	4	5	6	7	8	9	10	11	12	13	14	15	16	17	18
1	H																	He
2	Li	Be											B	C	N	O	F	Ne
3	Na	Mg											Al	Si	P	S	Cl	Ar
4	K	Ca	Sc	Ti	V	Cr	Mn	Fe	Co	Ni	Cu	Zn	Ga	Ge	As	Se	Br	Kr
5	Rb	Sr	Y	Zr	Nb	Mo	Tc	Ru	Rh	Pd	Ag	Cd	In	Sn	Sb	Te	I	Xe
6	Cs	Ba	*	Hf	Ta	W	Re	Os	Ir	Pt	Au	Hg	Tl	Pb	Bi	Po	At	Rn
7	Fr	Ra	**	Rf	Db	Sg	Bh	Hs	Mt	Uun	Uuu	Uub						

*	La	Ce	Pr	Nd	Pm	Sm	Eu	Gd	Tb	Dy	Ho	Er	Tm	Yb	Lu
**	Ac	Th	Pa	U	Np	Pu	Am	Cm	Bk	Cf	Es	Fm	Md	No	Lr

* Lanthanide metals
** Actinide metals

Key
Symbol
Atomic Number

It's "Element"ary! *(cont.)*

Producing the Projects *(cont.)*

Project 4—The Periodic Table—Discovering When the Elements Were Discovered

Provide students with a copy of *The Periodic Table—Discovery Dates* activity sheet that is shown on the following page. *The Periodic Table—Discovery Dates* activity sheet is available on the CD-ROM [filename: discover.doc]. There is also a *Discovery Dates Answer Key* available for your use on the CD-ROM [filename: discovan.doc].

Complete *The Periodic Table—Discovery Dates* as a class or allow pairs of students to work together to fill in the discovery date for each element on the computer system in your classroom or in the computer lab. If students are working in pairs, have them complete the following:

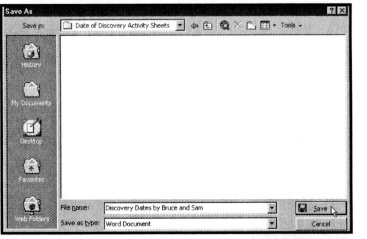

- Open *The Periodic Table—Discovery Dates* activity sheet.

- Before entering any data, click on the **FILE** menu and pull down to *Save As*. (This way, the activity sheet will remain intact.)

- Navigate to the folder where your teacher has told you to save your file.

- Change the filename to *Discovery Dates* with your names at the end, such as *Discovery Dates by Bruce and Sam*.

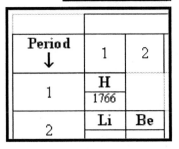

- Then click on the **Save** button.

- Now that you have saved the activity file as your very own, you can enter data.

- Click in the cell below the **H** for hydrogen.

- Type in the year that hydrogen was discovered, which is **1766**.

Period ↓	1	2
1	**H** 1766	
2	Li	Be

Special Note: Some of the elements were known by ancient civilizations; however, we don't know the exact dates the elements were discovered. For each of these elements, simply place an **A** in the cell for the date, indicating that it was known during **ancient times**.

Another Special Note: To move from cell to cell, you can click your mouse in the new cell, use the **<Tab>** key on your keyboard to move to the new cell, or use the arrow keys on your keyboard to move to the new cell. Do not press **<Enter>** or **<Return>** on your keyboard. This key only increases the number of lines in your cell. (If you pressed **<Enter>** or **<Return>** by mistake, simply press the **<Backspace>** or **<Delete>** key on your keyboard to remove the extra line(s) in the cell.)

- Click in the cell below the **He** for helium. Type in the year this element was discovered.

- Continue in this manner until your periodic table has all the discovery dates you could find.

- Be sure to save your work from time to time while typing and then again when you are finished. To save your file, click on the **Save** button on the **Standard Toolbar**.

It's "Element"ary! *(cont.)*

The Periodic Table
Discovering When the Elements Were Discovered

Directions: Below its symbol, fill in the date each element was discovered. If the element was discovered during ancient times and there is no specific date of discovery, enter an A for the date.

← **Group** →

Period	1	2	3	4	5	6	7	8	9	10	11	12	13	14	15	16	17	18
1	H																	He
2	Li	Be											B	C	N	O	F	Ne
3	Na	Mg											Al	Si	P	S	Cl	Ar
4	K	Ca	Sc	Ti	V	Cr	Mn	Fe	Co	Ni	Cu	Zn	Ga	Ge	As	Se	Br	Kr
5	Rb	Sr	Y	Zr	Nb	Mo	Tc	Ru	Rh	Pd	Ag	Cd	In	Sn	Sb	Te	I	Xe
6	Cs	Ba	*	Hf	Ta	W	Re	Os	Ir	Pt	Au	Hg	Tl	Pb	Bi	Po	At	Rn
7	Fr	Ra	**	Rf	Db	Sg	Bh	Hs	Mt	Uun	Uuu	Uub						

*	La	Ce	Pr	Nd	Pm	Sm	Eu	Gd	Tb	Dy	Ho	Er	Tm	Yb	Lu
**	Ac	Th	Pa	U	Np	Pu	Am	Cm	Bk	Cf	Es	Fm	Md	No	Lr

* Lanthanide metals
** Actinide metals

Key
Symbol
Atomic Number

It's "Element"ary! *(cont.)*

Producing the Projects *(cont.)*

Project 5—Grasping the Element Groups

Divide students into nine small research groups. Assign or have students select one of the following element groups to research:

- Alkali Metals
- Alkaline Earth Metals
- Transition Metals
- Other Metals
- Metalloids
- Non-Metals
- Halogens
- Noble Gases
- Rare Earth Elements

Provide each student group with copies of the *Grasping the Element Groups* activity sheet that is partially shown on the following page. The *Grasping the Element Groups* activity sheet file is available on the CD-ROM [filename: grasping.doc].

Allow each group to work together to gather the element group information and enter it into the computer system in your classroom or in the computer lab. Have students complete the following:

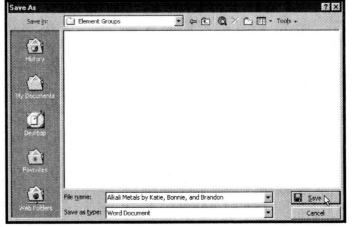

- Open the *Grasping the Element Groups* activity sheet file.

- Before entering any data, click on the **FILE** menu and pull down to *Save As*. (This way, the activity sheet will remain intact.)

- Navigate to the folder where your teacher has told you to save your file.

- Change the filename to reflect the element group you are researching, such as *Alkali Metals*. Place with your names at the end, such as *Alkali Metals by Katie, Bonnie, and Brandon*.

- Then click on the **Save** button.

- Now that you have saved the activity file as your very own, you can enter data.

- Carefully follow the instructions provided.

- Be sure to save your work from time to time while typing and then again when you are finished. To save your file, click on the **Save** button on the **Standard Toolbar**.

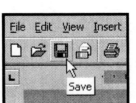

Directions: Follow the instructions provide

1. Highlight and bold the **Element Group** group to select (highlight) it. Then click on
   - **Alkali Metals**
   - Alkaline Earth Metals
   - Transition Metals
   - Other Metals
   - Metalloids

2. List the elements that are in your elemen Here's how: Click to the right of the bullet on your keyboard. You will automatically group. **Special Note:** If you are listing the
   - Lithium (Li)
   - Sodium (Na)
   - Potassium (K)
   - Rubidium (Rb)
   - Cesium (Cs)
   - Francium (Fr)

It's "Element"ary! *(cont.)*

Grasping the Element Groups

Directions: Follow the instructions provided in each cell of the table below.

1. Highlight and bold the Element Group that your team is assigned to research. Here's how: Click and drag across the element group to select (highlight) it. Then click on the **Bold** button on the **Formatting Toolbar**.

   - Alkali Metals
   - Alkaline Earth Metals
   - Transition Metals
   - Other Metals
   - Metalloids

   - Non-Metals
   - Halogens
   - Noble Gases
   - Rare Earth Elements

2. List the elements that are in your element group below. After each element, type its symbol in parenthesis, such as *Lithium (Li)*. Here's how: Click to the right of the bullet you see below. Type one element name and its symbol and press **<Enter>** or **<Return>** on your keyboard. You will automatically see a second bullet for your next element. Continue entering all the elements in your group. **Special Note:** If you are listing the Transition Metals, you will need to use both columns of bullets because there are so many.

•	•

3. List three to five characteristics of your element group below. Here's how: Click to the right of the bullet you see below. Type one characteristic of your element group. Then press **<Enter>** or **<Return>** on your keyboard. You will automatically see a second bullet for your next characteristic. Continue entering characteristics of your element group until your assignment is complete.

   -

4. On the **Periodic Table** on the following page, find the elements that are in your element group and shade them your team's favorite color. Here's how: Click in the cell containing one of the elements in your element group. Click on the **TABLE** menu, pull down to *Select*, and then select **Cell**. Next, click on the **FORMAT** menu and pull down to *Borders and Shading*. At the **Borders and Shading** window, click on the **Shading** tab to bring it to the forefront if it is not already there. Under the **Fill** color palette, click on your team's favorite color and then click **OK**.

   Special Note: If you do not see your team's favorite color, click on the **More Colors** button. At the **Colors** window, you can click on the **Standard** tab, select a color for the palette, and click **OK;** or you can click on the **Custom** tab, mix a custom color, and click **OK**. Continue shading the cells for the elements in your element group until your assignment is complete.

   Another Special Note: If you have elements in adjacent cells, select all the cells together to shade several at one time.

It's "Element"ary! *(cont.)*

Producing the Projects *(cont.)*

Project 5 *(cont.)*

Special Note: There is an answer key for each element group available on the CD-ROM. The files are *Grasping the Element Groups—Answer Key—Alkali Metals* [filename: alkali.doc], *Grasping the Element Groups—Answer Key—Alkaline Earth Metals* [filename: alkaline.doc], *Grasping the Element Groups—Answer Key—Transition Metals* [filename: transiti.doc], *Grasping the Element Groups—Answer Key—Other Metals* [filename: othermet.doc], *Grasping the Element Groups—Answer Key—Metalloids* [filename: metalloi.doc], *Grasping the Element Groups—Answer Key—Non-Metals* [filename: nonmetal.doc], *Grasping the Element Groups—Answer Key—Halogens* [filename: halogens.doc], *Grasping the Element Groups—Answer Key—Noble Gases* [filename: nobelgas.doc], and *Grasping the Element Groups—Answer Key—Rare Earth Elements* [filename: rareearth.doc].

Presenting the Projects

- Have students place the activity sheets in their science notebooks to keep as references.

- Display a selection of your students' completed periodic tables or research findings on a bulletin board or wall of your classroom.

- If your students researched the element groups, have each group report their findings to the class. Then discuss with students the characteristics of the element groups that make them unique.

Additional Project Ideas

- Have each student select and research one element, such as Uranium. Students can find out fun and interesting information about this element. For example, Uranium was named after the planet Uranus. It is a soft, silvery solid. Uranium is also radioactive!

- Have students create a *The Discovery of Elements Timeline*. There is a sample *The Discovery of Elements Timeline* available on the CD-ROM [filename: eletime.doc].

- Now that students have lots of information about the elements, divide students into small groups (3–4 students each). Have each group create an Elements Game. Whether it is a simple search-and-find activity sheet or an elaborate board game, students will have fun challenging each other with information about the elements.

- You can adapt one of the periodic table template files and have your students gather information about the freezing point of each element, the boiling point of each element, the color of each element, the mass of each element, and more.

Additional Resources

- There are several books that can provide information for your students' research into the element groups or families. An excellent book is *The Periodic Table* by Brian Knapp (published in 1998 by Grolier Educational, ISBN 0-7172-9149-9).

- A great Internet site that provides information about the elements can be found at:

http://www.chemicalelements.com

CD-ROM Index

Page Number in Text	Name of Project	Title of the File	Description	Filename on the CD-ROM
4	Introduction	*Additional Resources*	Resource file	addrsorc.doc
8	Iconic Story Writing	*The Little Lost Kitten*	Iconic story sample	lostkitn.doc
10	Iconic Story Writing	*Iconic Story Template*	Iconic story template	icontemp.doc
11	Open House Announcement	*Twin Peaks School Open House Announcement*	Open House Announcement Sample	openhous.doc
14	Open House Announcement	*Planning Our Open House Announcement*	Student activity sheets	planopen.doc
17	Open House Announcement	*Writing Process Tracking Sheet for the Open House Announcement*	Student activity sheet	writproc.doc
19	Super Spelling Triangles	*My Spelling Triangles Sample*	Sample student file	spellsam.doc
23	Super Spelling Triangles	*My Spelling Triangles Template*	Student file template	spelltem.doc
25	Making Math Tables	*Multiplication Table*	Resource file	multable.doc
28	Making Math Tables	*Multiplication Table Template*	Multiplication table template	multemp.doc
28	Making Math Tables	*Addition Table*	Resource file	addtable.doc
28	Making Math Tables	*Addition Table Template*	Addition table template	addtemp.doc
30	Creating Fraction Games	*Equivalent Fractions Shapes*	Resource file	equivshp.doc
34	Creating Fraction Games	*Equivalent Fractions Cards Samples*	Resource file	eqfracsm.doc
34	Creating Fraction Games	*Concentration Cards Template*	Template file	conctemp.doc
34	Creating Fraction Games	*Fraction to Decimal Conversions Cards*	Resource file	fradecc.doc
39	Comparing Native Americans	*A Comparison of Native Americans*	Research organizer template	natamtem.doc
39	Comparing Native Americans	*A Comparison of Pueblo and Chinook Homes*	Research organizer sample	natamsam.doc
41	Comparing Native Americans	*Comparing Native Americans Sample*	Presentation sample	nampresm.ppt
42	Comparing Native Americans	*Comparing Native Americans*	Presentation template	nampretm.ppt
46	Collecting Histories Through Timelines	*My Life Timeline Sample*	Sample timeline	tmlnsamp.doc
48	Collecting Histories Through Timelines	*My Life Timeline Template*	Timeline template	tmlntemp.doc
55	Collecting Histories Through Timelines	*The Life of Someone Special Timeline Template*	Timeline template	someone.doc
58	Collecting Histories Through Timelines	*The Life of a Famous Person Timeline Template*	Timeline template	person.doc
59	Collecting Histories Through Timelines	*Inventions Timeline Sample*	Sample timeline	inventsa.doc
60	Collecting Histories Through Timelines	*Invention Information Sheet Sample*	Sample information sheet	invinfos.doc

CD-ROM Index

Page Number in Text	Name of Project	Title of the File	Template Description	template Filename on the CD-ROM
60	Collecting Histories Through Timelines	*Invention Information Sheet Template*	Information sheet	invinfot.doc
64	Collecting Histories Through Timelines	*The Screw Invention Template*	template Invention	screw.doc
64	Collecting Histories Through Timelines	*The Printing Press Invention Template*	template Invention	printing.doc
64	Collecting Histories Through Timelines	*The Shirt Invention Template*	template Invention	shirt.doc
64	Collecting Histories Through Timelines	*The Bottle Cork Invention Template*	template Invention	bottlec.doc
64	Collecting Histories Through Timelines	*The Pencil Invention Template*	template Invention	pencil.doc
64	Collecting Histories Through Timelines	*The Telescope Invention Template*	template Invention	telescop.doc
64	Collecting Histories Through Timelines	*The Thermometer Invention Template*	template Invention	thermome.doc
64	Collecting Histories Through Timelines	*The Merry-Go-Round Invention Template*	template Invention	merry-go.doc
64	Collecting Histories Through Timelines	*The Calculator Invention Template*	template Invention	calculat.doc
64	Collecting Histories Through Timelines	*The Submarine Invention Template*	template Invention	submarin.doc
64	Collecting Histories Through Timelines	*The Umbrella Invention Template*	template Invention	umbrella.doc
64	Collecting Histories Through Timelines	*The Megaphone Invention Template*	template Invention	megaphon.doc
64	Collecting Histories Through Timelines	*The Pocket Watch Invention Template*	template Invention	pocketwa.doc
64	Collecting Histories Through Timelines	*The Piano Invention Template*	template Invention	piano.doc
64	Collecting Histories Through Timelines	*The Baby Carriage Invention Template*	template Invention	babycarr.doc
64	Collecting Histories Through Timelines	*The Lightening Rod Invention Template*	template Invention	lighteni.doc
64	Collecting Histories Through Timelines	*The Sextant Invention Template*	template Invention	sextant.doc
64	Collecting Histories Through Timelines	*Bifocal Eyeglasses Invention Template*	template Invention	bifocale.doc
64	Collecting Histories Through Timelines	*The Ambulance Invention Template*	template Invention	ambulanc.doc
64	Collecting Histories Through Timelines	*The Cotton Gin Invention Template*	template Invention	cottongi.doc
64	Collecting Histories Through Timelines	*The Battery Invention Template*	template Invention	battery.doc
64	Collecting Histories Through Timelines	*The Gas Stove Invention Template*	template Invention	gasstove.doc
64	Collecting Histories Through Timelines	*Canned Food Invention Template*	template Invention	cannedfo.doc
64	Collecting Histories Through Timelines	*The Sewing Machine Invention*	template Invention	

CD-ROM Index

Page Number in Text	Name of Project	Title of the File	Description	Filename on the CD-ROM
64	Collecting Histories Through Timelines	*The Lawnmower Invention Template*	Invention template	lawnmowe.doc
64	Collecting Histories Through Timelines	*The Bicycle Invention Template*	Invention template	bicycle.doc
64	Collecting Histories Through Timelines	*Anesthetics Invention Template*	Invention template	anesthet.doc
64	Collecting Histories Through Timelines	*The Saxophone Invention Template*	Invention template	saxophon.doc
64	Collecting Histories Through Timelines	*The Can Opener Invention Template*	Invention template	canopene.doc
64	Collecting Histories Through Timelines	*The Automobile Invention Template*	Invention template	automobi.doc
64	Collecting Histories Through Timelines	*The Zipper Invention Template*	Invention template	zipper.doc
64	Collecting Histories Through Timelines	*The Bulldozer Invention Template*	Invention template	bulldoze.doc
64	Collecting Histories Through Timelines	*Color Television Invention Template*	Invention template	colortel.doc
64	Collecting Histories Through Timelines	*The Helicopter Invention Template*	Invention template	helicopt.doc
64	Collecting Histories Through Timelines	*The Computer Invention Template*	Invention template	computer.doc
64	Collecting Histories Through Timelines	*Inventions Timeline Template*	Timeline template	inventte.doc
66	Collecting Histories Through Timelines	*Our School Year Timeline Template*	Timeline template	timsch.doc
71	Science Vocabulary Words—Find 'Em, Match 'Em, and Unscramble 'Em	*The Oceans Vocabulary Words—Find 'Em*	Sample activity sheet	ocnfdsa.doc
71	Science Vocabulary Words—Find 'Em, Match 'Em, and Unscramble 'Em	*The Oceans Vocabulary Words—Find 'Em Answer Key*	Activity sheet answer key	ocnfdak.doc
72	Science Vocabulary Words—Find 'Em, Match 'Em, and Unscramble 'Em	*The Oceans Vocabulary Words—Match 'Em*	Sample activity sheet	ocnmasa.doc
72	Science Vocabulary Words—Find 'Em, Match 'Em, and Unscramble 'Em	*The Oceans Vocabulary Words—Match 'Em Answer Key*	Activity sheet answer key	ocnmaak.doc
72	Science Vocabulary Words—Find 'Em, Match 'Em, and Unscramble 'Em	*The Oceans Vocabulary Words—Unscramble 'Em*	Sample activity sheet	ocnscsa.doc
72	Science Vocabulary Words—Find 'Em, Match 'Em, and Unscramble 'Em	*The Oceans Vocabulary Words—Unscramble 'Em Answer Key*	Activity sheet answer key	ocnscak.doc
72	Science Vocabulary Words—Find 'Em, Match 'Em, and Unscramble 'Em	*Vocabulary Words—Find 'Em Template*	Activity sheet template	vocfdtem.doc
75	Science Vocabulary Words—Find 'Em, Match 'Em, and Unscramble 'Em	*Vocabulary Words—Match 'Em Template*	Activity sheet template	vocmatem.doc

CD-ROM Index

Page Number in Text	Name of Project	Title of the File		Description
77	Science Vocabulary Words—Find 'Em, Match 'Em, and Unscramble 'Em	*Vocabulary Words—Unscramble 'Em Template*		Activity sheet template
80	It's "Element"ary!—Learning About the Periodic Table	*The Periodic Table of the Elements*		Resource file
82	It's "Element"ary!—Learning About the Periodic Table	*Element Names and Symbols*		Activity sheet
82	It's "Element"ary!—Learning About the Periodic Table	*Element Names and Symbols Answer Key*		Answer key
84	It's "Element"ary!—Learning About the Periodic Table	*The Periodic Table—It's "Element"ary*		Activity sheet
86	It's "Element"ary!—Learning About the Periodic Table	*The Periodic Table—Absent Atomic Numbers*		Activity sheet
88	It's "Element"ary!—Learning About the Periodic Table	*The Periodic Table—Discovery Dates*		Activity sheet
88	It's "Element"ary!—Learning About the Periodic Table	*Discover Dates Answer Key*		Answer key
90	It's "Element"ary!—Learning About the Periodic Table	*Grasping the Element Groups*		Activity sheet
92	It's "Element"ary!—Learning About the Periodic Table	*Grasping the Element Groups— Answer Key—Alkali Metals*		Answer key
92	It's "Element"ary!—Learning About the Periodic Table	*Grasping the Element Groups— Answer Key—Alkaline Earth Metals*		Answer key
92	It's "Element"ary!—Learning About the Periodic Table	*Grasping the Element Groups— Answer Key—Transition Metals*		Answer key
92	It's "Element"ary!—Learning About the Periodic Table	*Grasping the Element Groups— Answer Key—Other Metals*		Answer key
92	It's "Element"ary!—Learning About the Periodic Table	*Grasping the Element Groups— Answer Key—Metalloids*		Answer key
92	It's "Element"ary!—Learning About the Periodic Table	*Grasping the Element Groups— Answer Key—Non-Metals*		Answer key
92	It's "Element"ary!—Learning About the Periodic Table	*Grasping the Element Groups— Answer Key—Halogens*		Answer key
92	It's "Element"ary!—Learning About the Periodic Table	*Grasping the Element Groups— Answer Key—Noble Gases*		Answer key
92	It's "Element"ary!—Learning About the Periodic Table	*Grasping the Element Groups— Answer Key—Rare Earth Elements*		Answer key
92	It's "Element"ary!—Learning About the Periodic Table	*The Discovery of Elements Timeline*		Sample timeline